A Course in Prosperity

A 40-Day Manual for Masters of Prosperity

Julie Dankovich

Copyright © 2015 Julie Dankovich
All rights reserved.

ISBN-13: 978-1508721796
ISBN-10: 1508721793

For Dorothea Moreland.

"Until one is committed, there is hesitancy, the chance to draw back, always ineffectiveness. Concerning all acts of initiative (and creation) there is one elementary truth, the ignorance of which kills countless ideas and splendid plans: That the moment one definitely commits oneself, then Providence moves too. All sorts of things occur to help one that would never otherwise have occurred. A whole stream of events issue from the decision, raising in one's favor all manner of unforeseen incidents and meetings and material assistance, which no man could have dreamed would have come his way."
-W. H. Murray, The Scottish Himalayan Expedition

CONTENTS

A Course in Prosperity..i
Day 1 - Starting from Scratch 7
Day 2 - Goal Tending: An Essential Element for Creating Prosperity 10
Day 3 - Clarence, the Angel 14
Day 4 - The Mortal Mind: Our Command Center...18
Day 5 - 'In the Beginning...': The Gospel of Prosperity..20
Day 6 - The Blueprint of Your New Intriguing Life 25
Day 7 - Ordinary or Extraordinary: Which do you choose to be?...............................28
Day 8 - Affirmations: Say it is so, and it is. 31
Day 9 - Think and Grow Filthy Rich 35
Day 10 - Planting New Seeds in the Fertile Garden of Your Mind 38
Day 11 - The Magic Wand of Emotions 41
Day 12 - Speaking it into existence 45
Day 13 - Your Words Create Your World 49
Day 14 - The Art of Imagination 53
Day 15 - Like Attracts Like. Like it or Not. 57
Day 16 - Tapping into the Energy of Abundance. 60
Day 17 - Our Personal Energy Crisis 63
Day 18 - Man is a Machine 66
Day 19 - Having our emotions vs. being our emotions 70
Day 20 - The Divine Plan 74
Day 21 - All You Need is Love...77
Day 22 - You Are the Light. 81
Day 23 - I've Got that Joy, Joy, Joy, Joy Down in My Heart! 85
Day 24 - Childlike Wonder..89
Day 25 - Concentration Skills: Master This and You Can Create Absolutely Anything 93
Day 26 - A Wing and a Prayer...98
Day 27 – Synchronicities: Cosmic Coincidences...102
Day 28 – Paying Bills 107
Day 29 - Who We Are and Who We Can Become 111
Day 30 - Navy SEALS 115
Day 31 - Practice Makes Perfect. 119
Day 32 - An Attitude of Gratitude 122
Day 33 - A New View, A New You. Tah-Dah! 126
Day 34 - The 50-Million-Dollar Race Horse..130
Day 35 - Clap If You Believe! 134
Day 36 - The Emancipation of a Life of Struggle..138
Day 37 - Lions, and Tigers, and Bears...Oh My! 142
Day 38 - Lighten Up a Little, Will You? Geeze. 145

Day 39- Becoming a Pollyanna...149
Day 40 - It's a Wonderful Life 153
About the Author: 157

A COURSE IN PROSPERITY

Prosperity: the state of flourishing, thriving success or good fortune.
"There is only one way by which you can achieve prosperity. It is to take charge of your mind."
-Rev. Eric Butterworth

Your days of financial struggle are over.

A Course in Prosperity will change your life and your material circumstances forever. It is a 40-day program, a formula for change, success and achievement that will produce miraculous results in your life. Within this instructional manual are the tools and techniques with which to transform your life of financial struggle into a life of abundance. You'll make optimal use of your mind by re-training the very way in which you think about money and it will cause you to become magnetic to abundance. *This is a book that is to be used and not just read.* Do the daily work and you'll be met with an extraordinary outcome.

The time is right now. The moment is here for you to take a quantum leap forward, to realize and seize the opportunity to financially thrive in life. The journey on which you are about to embark is not one for sissies. It takes guts, courage, commitment, and focused effort to move in a new direction, so there will be no more living at half throttle. You have awoken from the trance and are poised for magnificence. Your life-changing adventure has just begun.

I've applied all the principles of this book to create a life of abundance; I am living proof that this program works. Believe me. I have been where you are. Who I was years ago is vastly different from who I am now. When my marriage of 15 years bitterly came to an end in 1996, I had no source of income and absolutely no idea how to generate one. I'd been a stay-at-home mother of two boys. Mine was a trail of broken hearts steeped in low self-esteem, self-defeating thought patterns, and so much bitterness and anger. Woe was me. I always seemed to have more than enough dysfunction and drama in my life that ultimately left me feeling powerless and stuck. I recognize now that I was living my life by default, believing I had no ability to control anything that happened to me. Now I know much different. Thank God.

My husband, Frank, had always been the breadwinner, and he earned a decent living. He was the one who paid the bills and controlled all the finances. When our marriage ended, so did my financial security, and the emotional tug of war began. I felt alone and terrified that I'd end up a depressed single mother living in a shack on welfare. I was left with the mortgage and all the expenses that went along with it. I remember nights when I would turn off all the lights after my children went to bed and burn candles to save on my electric bill. I was barely eating. I was a walking nerve end and as depressed as I'd ever been. I never wanted my children to know how viciously this tormenting fear of poverty was overtaking my life. That alone provided me with the tenacity, courage and motivation to put into place a daily routine of practicing all the principles in this book, and I changed my life permanently. Heaven knows I desperately needed it.

My divorce was the catalyst that spurred me into action. Once I set my mind to creating a new life of financial freedom, there was no turning back. I made the decision not to be a victim, and because of the work I did on reprogramming my behavior and the way my mind thought about money, I no longer struggle financially. I have more than enough money to live the life of my dreams. I caused a significant shift to occur in my financial circumstances by doing this work, and you can too. You are no different than me. It's time to rediscover yourself. Perhaps you have forgotten: You are strong, lionhearted, and full of zest and pluck. You *can* have an astonishing life of overflowing prosperity, goodness, and joy. The materials and direction are right here in your very hands, and the results will be exponential. It's never too late to have the life of your dreams. Never.

What you can expect as a result of working this program:
- A new financial mind set will emerge. Your income will increase, and you'll experience sudden and consistent windfalls of money - checks will unexpectedly arrive in the mail; you'll be offered things for free; you'll randomly find money, etc. You'll become lucky in all facets of life.
- You'll feel exceptionally happier on a daily basis. Happiness breeds happiness, and happiness breeds abundance in all areas of life. Prepare to have your world rocked.
- Extraordinary peace of mind will be yours.
- You'll become quite adept at creating anything you want in life, and it will blow your mind.
- You'll stop planning and start executing, and high-caliber performance will be the result.

We feel we have failed at life, but that's been an illusion all along- a self-created nightmare. Our mystical heritage has been forgotten. We have within us real power to bring forth prosperity, and it's time to reclaim our mystical past and our spiritual glory. It doesn't matter how many times we've botched things up in the past. It doesn't matter if we've suffered significant financial disasters, like a bankruptcy or a home eviction. There is a power far greater than ourselves, and it's waiting to be tapped into. This colossal power under our control is a power greater than poverty, greater than a lack of education, greater than being a product of a dysfunctional childhood, greater than all of our fears, life dramas, self doubts, and beliefs combined. It is the power to take control of your own mind and direct it to the success you so desire. The enormous power of the mind is a gift from God. It's the most magnificent gift to human beings, and it is *the only thing* over which you have the complete and unchallengeable right of control and direction. When you think or speak of your lack of money or income, you are simply enforcing that lack by directing the great power of the mind to attract the adverse circumstances to you. *It is absolutely true that whatever your mind dwells upon is precisely what appears in your life.* This is why it is absolutely essential that you recognize and believe that all success begins with a clear and precise picture in the mind of exactly what you want from life.

Each and every one of us has been blessed with the ability of controlling our mind power and directing it to whatever ends we choose. You simply haven't practiced it enough to be any good at it yet. God does not care how you live your life. God gave you power to create anything you want, and it makes absolutely no difference to Him what you create. You get to be, do and have whatever you want. You can choose whether you live an ordinary life or an extraordinary sacred experience. Free will allows you to choose it all. God created you. You created the rest, and you created it with the power you have within.

It's as though at birth, you're given two sealed envelopes. One of the envelopes is clearly labeled, *"The extraordinary and deeply fulfilling life you will enjoy if you take control of your own mind and direct it towards creating heaven on earth."* Within this envelope, is a detailed list of the regular occurrence of miracles that fulfill every dream you've ever dreamt. The lavish trips you'll take. The beautiful home you'll easily afford. The money you'll use to bless the lives of others. The second envelope is marked, *"The suffering you will endure in life if you neglect to take control of your own mind and intentionally direct it."* Within this envelope is a list detailing the piles of bills marked "Final Notice," the car that always breaks down, the meager house you could barely afford, and the stress, anxiety, and bitterness associated with the lack you constantly experience as a result of not directing your mind in a way that creates a life you absolutely love. Which envelope have you opened?

How this program works:

Wealth is a mindset. We're either attracting money or repelling it. While material abundance is certainly not the most important thing in life, financial burdens are vicious barriers that keep our greatness at bay. They not only rob us of peace of mind, but they negatively impact our relationships, even the way we parent. We subsist on a hotbed of negativity, martyrs to the victimization of a negative mind, which impedes our ability to soar. In this program, you'll be turning inward to create the abundance you've been waiting, praying, and hoping for. You'll become quite adept at manifesting anything you want, and it will blow your mind, I swear.

You want the bottom line here? Schedule the same times daily to do the work, and you will be met with the miraculous financial breakthrough of a lifetime. The principles of this book involve powers you already possess. They are the powers of deliberate thought, emotion, spoken word, and imagination. By repeatedly and intentionally focusing on abundance on a daily basis, the liberation from financial peril occurs. Thoughts, if powerful enough, are accepted by our subconscious mind, and they influence our daily experience.

Financial abundance is an internal matter, and you're going to learn why. This is the operator's manual for your brain. Your sufferings are the result of negative money brain patterns you've developed over the course of a lifetime. Our brains learn quickly with patterns and repetition. When we concentrate on specific thoughts, the neurons in the brain create a pathway that remembers the thought pattern on which we're focusing our attention. The brain is best able to memorize what it is experiencing through concentration and focus. With the consistent and intentional repetition of new thoughts about money combined with the mastery of your emotions, spoken words, and imagination, prosperity shall be yours.

Read this manual every day, without fail, to keep your focus where it needs to be: on abundance. You'll implement a daily routine using the techniques outlined here to override the old, limiting money beliefs that have been running rampant in your mind. The level and speed to which you succeed at achieving financial success will depend on the level and frequency of attention you place on prosperity. If you really want to make a speedy and drastic change in your income, spend more than the recommended amount of time doing the exercises.

You'll be injecting playfulness into this work, so your experience of it will be unbridled bliss. I promise you that. This work is a real life-changer. What you'll be doing is consciously designing your life, and it'll be like pulling rabbits from a hat--magical, mystical, and miraculous.

Continue along the path you've been on and do nothing to change your beliefs and behaviors related to money and personal finance, and the probable almost certain outcome is that you'll continue to struggle financially for the remainder of your life. Nothing is wrong with that. It is what it is. Or perhaps you could simply choose different actions that produce different results: results in which prosperity occurs for you easily, where stunning happiness and radical self-fulfillment are daily occurrences. You can radically alter your life by making new choices of thought that direct you towards prosperity and abundance instead of repelling it.

Oh, how we itch for the big score. We buy lottery tickets. We want a wealthy somebody to whisk us far, far away from whatever disaster we're reeling from at the moment. We're convinced we cannot do it for ourselves. We wait in desperate anticipation for money to fall from the sky and into our lucky little laps. Do we actually believe that if we do nothing different, our financial circumstances will alter? No, no, my friend. This canon is quite different. No one else can save us, deliver us, or provide us with the desperate salvation we seek from our fractured finances. Do not fall asleep and miss your life! Maybe, just maybe, you can begin to believe in miracles again. The secret here is this: By doing the daily prosperity work, heaven on earth will appear. This is your opportunity to be cause in the matter. Commit to the daily work, and *you will begin to thrive financially*. Trust that with practice, you will successfully disable your habitual patterns of lack and struggle.

Being alive is a great and deep privilege. We are no accident, lacking an enduring purpose. Far from it. We are the clearing to make manifest the grandeur of God who is within us. You're on your own path to put a dent in this great big world. Gratefully, you *can* begin again. This is your chance. Heed the priceless wisdom within the prosperous envelope you were offered at birth. It's being offered once again, only this time you're paying attention. This is the tipping point from which you choose to be extraordinary for the remainder of your life. Applause, please.

How to use *A Course in Prosperity*:
You're investing in yourself. By employing the skills outlined in this manual with great frequency for a period of time, you will disrupt your seemingly endless struggle with money. All that is required is intentionality, concentration, daily repetition, and the willingness to be the very best version of yourself. You'll begin to live each day with efficiency and clarity of purpose. This field manual provides you the access for true financial transformation. By making the time and taking the time, your prosperity work will be scheduled into your daily routine. Without fail, you will carve out just 10-20 minutes twice each day, to do the work. The brain is receptive to patterns, and this routine powerfully trains your mind with the new thought process that will generate your financial success. Spending more time is highly recommended if you want to see dramatic results, but 20-30 minutes is the minimum amount of time you should invest daily.

The program works best if you spend 10-15 minutes in the morning, so you begin your day big. Before you go to sleep at night, you'll spend another 10-15 minutes, so the last thoughts you have before drifting off to sleep are those that will be creating your new life of prosperity.

I recommend you practice your prosperity efforts at the same times each day, and hold those time slots as sacred space because they are. While I was in training for abundance, I carved out interludes of solitude upon waking and before I went to bed every single day. This was my training post, the devoted time I used to practice the mental exercises that coaxed all of my hopes, my dreams, and my wishes into physical reality.

Your Daily Assignment:
- Read the daily passage, preferably first thing in the morning.
- Take at least 10-15 minutes in the morning and at least 10-15 minutes in the evening to practice using the tools outlined in this course.
- Create daily goals.
- List at least three things for which you are grateful.

Plan your work and work your plan.

This is a key element of the program. *Schedule the time necessary to do the work and make a firm commitment to honor that schedule.* Re-read that last sentence, please. It is the key to your financial salvation. Since the program works by conditioning your mind to attract abundance, I cannot stress enough how important it is to develop the daily discipline to work the program. Like any new skill, it takes practice, practice, practice, and soon you will powerfully draw abundance into your life. Nevertheless, if you only practice the skills for a mere five minutes each day, you'll be better off than not doing it at all. Do what you can when you can. Go ahead, say it. You're already running frazzled as it is, right? If you don't plan the time to do the exercises, you'll be scrambling to fit them into your already-hectic life, and the effort you put into this program dictates the results you will get. The more effort you put in, the more successful you'll be in getting the income you desire. Remember, you'll be working diligently for the next several weeks to re-program your mind to attract money to you. After 40 days, the tools and techniques will become habitual for you, and you won't need to be as intentional about integrating them into your daily round.

You hold in your hands the manual for prosperity-the bible for masters of prosperity. Study the material, for it holds the secrets to your success, to your heart. Where your thinking is, there is your experience. You magnetize into your life whatever you hold in thought. What's going on around you is not reality. We are all waking dreamers. Our lives are like movies on a movie screen, and the projector is our imagination. The movie, our lives, is what we give permission to put into our imagination. You created the mess you're living in, and the time will come when you're swimming in your money. I'll teach you how prosperity works and how to control it. You'll have powers over the illusions of the mind because you'll know the reality behind them. We all know this information; we're simply unaware that we know, yet.

This is your opportunity to change from the inside out, to reinvent yourself and intentionally design every corner of your beautiful life. For the next 40 days, you'll be playing the money game. Play this game as if your life depends on it, because in reality, it actually does. Not having enough money stymies you from doing the things you want to do and having the things you want. The very quality of your life is greatly impacted by your lack of financial freedom. Remove the obstacle of never having enough money, and you can do and have essentially whatever you want.

I feel like I have ruled the world; it's time for you to rule yours. You've been shrinking yourself long enough. The day of awakening is upon you. Prepare to have hope reborn. Challenge yourself to go beyond where you've stopped before. You're swimming in a sea of endless possibility, so get ready to have your dreams come alive. There's no going back to sleep. There's no more schlepping through life. No siree. You are the bold creator of your destiny, and today begins the love affair with your life. You get to live the life of your dreams—dreams that set your soul on fire.

Are you ready to disappear the galaxies of struggle and lack that have kept your dreams at bay? I thought so. Let's get your party started, shall we? Just how much abundance can you stand?

> "Aim with your heart, steer with your mind, and know that it always works. Besides, aiming, without steering, is just daydreaming."
> **-Mike Dooley**

Day 1 - Starting from Scratch

"There's only one despair worse than 'God, I blew it,' and that's 'God, I blew it again." -Marianne Williamson

Everywhere, bills. And more bills. *'What new hell awaits me today?'* Your thoughts beg as you clamber out of bed. Careening from one crisis to another, our fragile lives come crashing down around us, and we're once again on our knees begging for the strength to survive the financial purgatories that never fail to frazzle and frighten. We don't seem to have the secret ingredient that others seem to have that enables them to live a life of freedom and ease, a life of financial abundance. The emotional undertow has been drowning us for far too long. Slowly and insidiously, the fears of financial failure dominate. The truth is we have no bloody idea how we ended up where we are, having been pulled along a tide more powerful than ourselves. We crave a miracle, a new beginning. We can remain who we are and sink further into the scourge of the troubled financial life we've already created for ourselves, or we can allow our hearts to break wide open, out of which our divine destiny emerges.

The emotional havoc we experience in this all-out war of just keeping our heads above water is now subsiding. Do you know why? *Because you are choosing to do something very different this time.* You are being cause in the matter of your own life, and it's going to be a ride of a lifetime. No longer do you dwell in the shadow of the valley of lost dreams and dashed hopes. Your dog days of suffering will soon be a faint and ashy memory. You are where you are in your finances right now, and it's absolutely perfect. Believe me; you can undo even the messiest and tangled demise. You *can* turn things around. New beginnings are possible for us all.

Your sufferings have been terrible. Know that my heart is full of compassion, affection, and love for you and where you've been. Days of faithlessness, doubt, and melancholic brooding, I've known them well. As my marriage was crumbling, I had never been so psychically and spiritually out of whack. I was at my weakest, convinced I'd been mis-delivered into a life that was too small to bear. Discouragement, denial, sadness, and self-doubt scraped the marrow of my soul as I grieved the death of my dreams; the death of hope, the death of trust. I wanted a second chance at my life but didn't know where to begin. I'd been emotionally residing in lower worlds, and I desperately yearned for ascension into higher realms. Mine was a sorrowful soul, but I was too paralyzed to take action. I experienced such disbelief that anything good could possibly happen for me, I'd actually made myself physically sick. I had little energy and even getting out of bed was a struggle. My thoughts were so dark and full of fear that I'd actually caused my white blood cell count to drop drastically. My primary physician sent me to see an oncologist, and at that point, I believed I was dying. My grandmother died of leukemia, so I knew that a drop in white blood cells was one of the indicators of that.

The oncologist I met with was a soft-spoken, petite Indian woman who carefully explained the poor results of my blood work to me, and I began to sob.

"I don't know what to do, I have no idea what to do..." The dam broke and I was drowning in my own fear. *"I have 2 children who need me, and I feel like a failure, like my life never really started. I'm so scared. Can you please help me? Please?"* I begged. I pleaded. I bawled.

She took my hand, looked into my eyes and said, *"Child, this could very well be something caused by a number of things. Do not be frightened. Our minds are very powerful. Do you know this? You have made yourself sick with so much worry and sadness, and you can surely make yourself well."*

"Do you meditate?" she asked. I told her I'd practiced meditation when I was in my twenties. *"Go home and begin meditating and ask God to bring you peace. This is important. Do this every day and don't allow concern to enter your mind. You'll know what to do to be happy and at peace. We'll do another blood test in a few weeks to see if there's improvement."*

This blew my mind. Shockingly, the truth had been revealed. Her compassion was so pure and tender; in her reassurance I found the direction I'd been seeking. I hadn't correlated my depressed state-of-mind with the collapse of my health until that day. My mental house of sadness had naively mis-created the nightmare I was living, and my doctor was strongly insinuating I could do something about it. The hopelessness that had been smothering me for years was now being lifted. Her prescription of meditation and creating peace of mind was the source of my recovery and the beginning of my salvation. I told Frank I was divorcing him, and so my journey of redefining who I was and how I lived my life began. I was standing at the crossroads of my future, and though the fear was still debilitating, I no longer cowered before it. The work outlined in this manual was what I put to use to not only restore the levels of my white blood cell count, but to create abundance, joy, and peace of mind that I'd never known before. It became an exploration into the unknown, and my financial transformation graciously became the genesis to the spiritual revolution that ensued.

I always shunned organized religion that was fear based, and I used to think I wasn't religious. My spiritual pursuit had always been sporadic, yet I desperately ached for a relationship to something profound, especially when my life went spinning so far out of control. What I know now is that my faith is internal, a mystical and profound bond that lifts me up and allows me to become far bigger than any pain and suffering.

It was never intended that anyone should be poor. You may not be destitute, but if you weren't suffering with your finances, you wouldn't have been drawn to this book. So how exactly did you end up where you are now? We feel like we work our fingers to the bone, only to find ourselves no farther advanced than we were before. We aren't earning enough money. Our homes are being foreclosed on. We're still living paycheck to paycheck, and we still struggle paying our bills. We believe we must work hard to achieve great success or overcome difficult times. Pssssst!! Y'all ready for this? *It is not true that we must work hard to achieve financial success.* The only effort you must make is to train your brain to attract abundance. By doing so, abundance will easily and effortlessly appear, and it will feel like pure magic. Keep reading. Each day you'll learn more about just how to make this happen.

You are not without blessing. You *can* recover. You *can* rise. And you *will* fly. It's a new day. The slate has been wiped clean. And I don't give two hoots if you've failed again, again, and yet again. Your past choices are unimportant. The many bumps and bruises you've experienced along the way were simply miracles disguised as struggles that had no other avenue of reaching you. There is no better time. This is your second chance. You're starting from scratch. Today is the day of demarcation as you journey towards the triumph of your travails. You're embarking on an unprecedented and exhilarating episodic expedition, and a profound inner shift will be the result.

Everything needed to begin you already have. There is immense abundance already within you. It's always been there for the asking, but all along you've believed it was too far out of your reach. Well, it's not. Within this field manual lie the mystical secrets that will alter the course of destiny. Give yourself permission to have a great life, will you? Something grand is waiting for you so get up, dress up, and show up. You're changing the way the game is played. It's a new day. A new you now arises in the world. Prepare to be delivered into the life you were meant for.

You have so many gifts hidden under your wings, and every gift needs unwrapping. Allow your spirit to fly free and dare to begin the adventure. It's time for a revival. You're embarking on your own personal resurrection from that which keeps you suffering, and you'll soon be grazing at life's all-you-can-eat buffet with breezy good cheer. You're not only going to amp your income, but more importantly, you will be far happier than you've ever been before. And by being so much happier, a bounty of goodness will flow freely into your life.

We miracle workers have to stick together, so let's do this thing. An exquisite journey is about to unfold, so enroll the stars to come out of the sky and light the path for you. Forty days from now, you will bear no resemblance to the person you were, and others will take notice. This is *so* your year!

How great I am.

I love my life!

I always have more than enough money to live comfortably.

All the money I want or need easily flows into my life.

There is more than enough to go around for everyone.

> "There comes a special moment in everyone's life, a moment for which that person was born. That special opportunity, when he seizes it, will fulfill his mission - a mission for which he is uniquely qualified. In that moment, he finds his greatness. It is his finest hour."
> **-Winston Churchill**

Day 2- Goal Tending: An Essential Element for Creating Prosperity

"A man without a plan for the day is lost before he starts." -Lewis K. Bendele

Give me an I.V. super espresso coffee drip, STAT! We major in busy and minor in overwhelm, don't we? The world is moving fast, so life seems to be more of a female dog metaphor than it is a pleasure to live. Simmering in quiet desperation from the exhausting lives we lead, we numb ourselves with designer pharmaceuticals that offer only temporary solace from the resignation, restlessness, and agitation of the emotional and financial debts we bear. We're a society of lost souls mired in financial drudgery. Our sighs speak volumes. We sense a buried, secret life waiting to be lived. We feel it in our bones. The truth is, we are all intended to shine, but how on earth do we live up to the magnificent potential that lies within when we can barely get through the day?

Those who are the wealthiest know how to harness the incredible power of their thoughts, desires, and determination. They never waver from their goals, nor do they allow anything or anyone to stop or deter them from achieving their goals. They desire, they focus, they imagine, they believe, and they take action; therefore, *they manifest*. Each one of us has this ability, if we choose it.

What's your life like right now? What are your finances like? Who are the people in your life? Are you in charge of your life? These are important questions to ask yourself to gauge exactly what you and you alone have created thus far. Your life is yours to control, to change, and to resolve what does not fit. The enemy is ourselves, not anyone else. We're constantly making choices and decisions that determine what our future will be, and we're making choices constantly whether we're aware of it or not. Our current circumstances are the result of mismanaged thoughts that run wildly and without direction leaving us living a life unconsciously with no deliberate purpose. What's been missing is intentionality with our choices. We choose the job we have, the way in which we spend our money, the way in which we save and grow our money, and we most certainly choose how we create money for ourselves. Whether we're aware of it or not, we are responsible for it all. We are the sum total of our choices, and our choices have been driven by a bankrupt brain pattern and untamed thoughts. This manual provides the tools for interrupting the brain patterns that no longer serve you. By doing so, you become the creative master you were born to be, but you must *choose* to use the tools consistently. The more intentional your choices are, the more you live your life on purpose. You can create absolutely anything you want in life when you have a daily game plan in place.

You are a divine change-maker. The time is ripe to take a quantum leap forward, to realize and seize the opportunity to thrive in all areas of life. Setting clear, specific, and positive goals provides the workable ground strategy that leads you down the yellow brick road to the magnificent destiny that's been waiting to be realized. This is the way.

There's unrelenting power in creating serious daily action items. They provide the road map to producing jaw-dropping, high-caliber performance. And you want a piece of that, don't you? When I started down the path of prosperity, I found that being highly organized made my life more efficient, less stressful, and far more productive. Goal setting was instrumental to my success and provided the necessary structures needed to maintain my discipline of utilizing these mind tools that eventually generated all sorts of abundance on a daily basis.

You're redesigning ever corner of your world, and you'll create it to look any way you want. Goal setting is the advanced scouting necessary for consciously nurturing our most beautiful dreams into fruition. It steadies the course. We are habitual in nature, so creating daily goals provides you with an agenda for creating the bigger life you were commissioned to live. Without actions there are no results. Each time we fall behind what we planned to do, another opportunity to shine passes. We'll use excuses and find reasons for not starting or completing tasks, but most of our excuses keep us from living a bigger life. Yours is a great mission, but the greater the mission, the greater the reward. It is the bigger challenges that really develop us.

How much of your day is carelessly spent watching TV, talking on the phone, surfing the Internet, or participating in numbing chatter about how the bad economy is? Turn off the TV, and refrain from watching the news and reading the newspaper for the next 40 days. You're re-programming your mind to attract great things to you, so it's vital that the negative messages in the media don't counteract with the positive work you'll be doing. You're going to be very intentional with your time, and for the next several weeks, your daily round will be well thought out and planned. Schedule 10-15 minutes every morning (wake up a little earlier than usual, if you must) and 10-15 minutes before drifting off to sleep at night to concentrate your mind power on the new positive money thoughts you're creating for yourself.

We're unorganized and don't finish what we start. Be aware of the impact that order, or the absence of it, plays in your life. It's not easy to think clearly when we're living in the midst of clutter and chaos. You're on an accelerated course of achievement, and goal setting will cause a quantum leap in your performance. You are the only one standing in your way. You can hang with the turkeys or soar with the eagles. You can watch a lot of TV, or you can choose to live a big life. The choice is yours alone. Most people are sleepwalking through life. You are not one of the walking dead. You are alive and filled with possibility.

From this day forward, choose to make this work your priority. Do something today that you've been afraid to do. Step out of your comfort zone. Get in action and get organized. Accomplish all that you've been procrastinating. You're embarking on a new path of financial liberty, so tackle the minutia that bogs you down. Appreciate the living that takes place in your home and begin to bring order there. Simplify. Get rid of the clutter. Get organized, and it won't simply be your domicile that gets transformed. Be impeccable with your car, your home, and your belongings. They're all a reflection of who you are. Each day, you'll be setting goals like cleaning your house, organizing your cupboards, weeding out the unflattering clothes that no longer make you feel like a million bucks. You are absolutely beautiful, so begin acting it.

Divest yourself of all the belongings you don't love and keep only the things you adore and simply can't live without. Make room for abundance and abundance will arrive. If you need some cash right now, sell the items you really don't want on eBay or craigslist. Get the oil changed in your car. Make the phone calls you've been too afraid to make. Get things moving that historically have never moved before in your life. Schedule the appointments you've been putting off. Organize your bills using a glitzy binder or folder that appeals to you. Create a resume that highlights just how brilliant you really are. List the tasks that you will complete each day—all of them—and keep these goals in view throughout the day, so you're present to what you're out to accomplish. And from this day forward, maintain your daily ritual of the mind work outlined in this manual, and you'll soon discover that order and a sense of accomplishment begin to take shape.

You are at one of the most significant crossroads of your entire life, for you are breaking out of the dense cocoon of lack, struggle, limitation, and exhaustion. It's time to step up your game. You'll be paying close attention to the choices you make. Seems wise? Well, it is.

It takes commitment and intentional effort to move in a new direction and alter your life permanently. To create order where there is none, begin with your daily goals. This is dire to your success, and there is no stopping the shift it will induce. Your daily goals outline the actions to get you exactly where you want to go.

The world will reflect back to you precisely what you predominantly focus on. You'll be practicing your wildly creative manifestation skills each day until you master them. To foster your own greatness, you'll want to center yourself often. Peace of mind is very serious business, so schedule a few minutes daily to spiritually retreat from the outer world that can distract. Meditation, prayer, or a solitary walk in nature never fails to provide a great release from the vicious cycle of negativity and chaos that hovers closely all too often, so consistently seek mental clarity in the silence.

You *are* the moves you make. You can create heaven or you can create hell. Which will it be? I thought so. I'll hold your hand. I'll take you home. You were born with a purpose. Reader, your life is about to change, so get ready to exceed your greatest expectations of yourself, of your life. Before you lays a vast ocean of infinite possibilities, and an impartial flow of universal abundance is just waiting to be tapped into. You are full of conviction. You are extraordinary, so have the audacity to shine, please. You have no idea how absolutely powerful you really are. I am in complete and utter awe of you.

And so we begin...

All the money I could possibly want is flowing towards me right now.

Each day my life gets better and better.

I am the master of matter.

> "Take five minutes to center yourself in the morning...set your intention every day...if you don't have five minutes, you don't deserve to have the life of your dreams."
> **– Oprah Winfrey**

TODAY'S GOALS

You're creating financial freedom, and goal setting is the foundation of it, you little genius, you. Creating daily goals generates tireless energy. They keep you on track. They reveal your gifts and talents. Prioritize everything in your daily routine and allow peace of mind to surface as you do so. List all the things you'll take action on today. By creating order out of mayhem and managing the many concerns and tasks that plague your mind, the lighter you will become.

- Getting up
- Dedlly working
- Balance budget assess damage
- Bath
- yard or kids clothes

- Jake cass

> "Go confidently in the direction of your dreams!
> Live the life you've imagined. As you simplify your
> life, the laws of the universe will be simpler."
> **-Henry David Thoreau**

THINGS FOR WHICH I'M GRATEFUL

You are irresistible, mysterious, smart, passionate and sassy. There is nothing you can't do. Instead of focusing on the empty spaces in your life, look for evidence of all the wonder that surrounds you. You were given the gift of another day. Look around. Take stock of it all. Allow your mind to stay centered on the things of light and love. Today, you are an optimist.

- my kids
- Daniella still being you

> "If you're bored with life — you don't get up every morning with
> a burning desire to do things — you don't have enough goals."
> **-Lou Holtz**

I am destined for greatness.

Day 3 - Clarence, the Angel

"We are not human beings having a spiritual experience. We are spiritual beings having a human experience." -Pierre Teilhard de Chardin

Reader, I ask you to keep an open mind with this work. It's the kiss of life. Everything about you is pure heaven. You've just forgotten that. You've become blind to your brilliance. You were drawn to this book, and you'll soon discover there are no accidents. It does not matter what your spiritual belief system is. We were all created from the same source. Whether you feel more comfortable calling this source God or the Universe or your Creator is completely up to you. I was raised Catholic, so I call our creator God. We come from love, so *we are love*. We are pure as rainwater. We are meant to thrive. We are endlessly creative, and life is intended to be magnificent for us all. But we've hit rock bottom so many times that our knees are shaky; our tender souls are bruised, our spirits broken. Blindsided by yet another crisis, we're weary and raw from the many financial missteps we've made. And the way in which we suffer from the endless slogging of the seemingly endless monetary breakdowns is in discord with who we really are.

We are mystical in nature; we *are* holy. As babies, we came joyously into this existence eager for the opportunity to create joyful experiences. This is our purpose. God created us so he could experience through us. We are meant to experience unspeakable joy, and we have unlimited and vastly creative capabilities. This is who we really are at our core; this *is* our natural state of being. Born with everything we need to know to thrive, we've somehow lost our way. We've forgotten just how enormously powerful we are, and from where we came. It's our humanity, our identity, our ego that gets in the way and causes all of our suffering. As we descended from Heaven to this earthly realm, the angels whispered softly to us, *"Once you're born, you'll forget everything you know about being an angel. You'll forget that you are powerful beyond measure. You'll forget from whence you came. But don't panic. It will slowly come back to you as you discover joy amid all the wonder and love that exists on earth. We'll protect you when you need protecting. And we'll be guiding you every step of the way. We will never leave your side. We're waiting to connect with you, coaxing you towards your dreams, so every one of your desires is fulfilled. You'll connect with us in the silence. "* And then we're born. The glaring lights and the harsh, cold environment are shocking. The confusion is so catapulting that we let out our first earthly cry, and our wispy ethereal memories are wiped clean.

Clarence Odbody is the fledgling guardian angel of George Bailey in Frank Capra's 1946 film *It's a Wonderful Life*. Clarence, an Angel Second Class, is tasked with a mission: prevent the suicide of a deeply troubled George Bailey, whose mounting personal and financial troubles have plunged him into an abyss of despair. If successful in his seraphic assignment, Clarence will finally earn his wings after more than 200 years of trying. The disheveled, clumsy angel-in-training is dispatched from Heaven, bumbling his way through the assignment, not yet having mastered his ethereal powers. But he has an idea.

"You've been given a great gift, George: a chance to see what the world would be like without you," Clarence tells the despondent and desperate man. And so the apprentice angel provides George with the grim view of the world without him in it. George has grossly underestimated all the good he has done as he witnesses firsthand the many lives he has impacted, the scores of

selfless contributions he has made to his community, and how very, very different and empty the world would be had he never been born. With a newfound appreciation of all the love, joy, and goodness that he'd been blind to before, George finally realizes that his is a wonderful life, and the ditsy angel at last earns his wings.

Consider that we are all very much like Clarence the angel. We are spiritual beings living in a clumsy human body with a complex human brain having a very human experience, and it ain't always pretty. We stumble—oh, how we fall—and life ends up occurring for us as if we are utterly powerless and have absolutely no control. But our buried treasure lies within. We are wildly creative masters; our mission is to create and experience profound joy. We are equipped with far more than our mortal minds. We are enormously powerful, yet we've had no idea how to access that power.

God gave each one of us the very same power to create that He has. There is profound love, light, and magnificent power within us because God put it there. It is eternally etched in our hearts, our souls. This is our cosmic function. We just haven't been using it to the best of our abilities. You're in training to master your power, so get ready to have your socks knocked off. A monumental shift in your finances is now in the works, and your life is about to change. You've been divinely gifted with free will and a powerful imagination that provides you with the full capability to be, do, and have absolutely anything you want in this lifetime. Your magical powers have been locked in the safe, and you've just found the key. You haven't yet seen the light that awaits.

Using only our mortal minds, we have very little access to create what we want to experience in life. We have within us extraordinary resources at our command: *the power of thought, the power of emotion, the power of our word, and the power of a rich imagination.* These are our magic wands, and we constantly use them to create every single one of our experiences—both good and bad. Most of the time we're unconsciously using them, but they're in continuous creation mode at all times, which is precisely why our lives look the way do, one financial disaster after another. We create constantly with our thoughts. Thought is cause. Experience is effect. Until now, we didn't know any better. Our wings were clipped; we've simply fallen victim to an untamed mortal mind. We're tapping into our angelic nature from here on out, and we'll be mastering our mighty magic wands.

Mastering the powerful gifts with which we've been blessed will require some practice. When we don't manage our thoughts or our emotions, we run the serious risk of having circumstances manifest that we didn't want to occur for us in the first place. Nothing can enter into our experience without our invitation. We create all of our experiences and circumstances with our wands of thought, emotion, conversation, and imagination. Period. We think and speak certain thoughts that cause us to feel certain emotions, and then we imagine the circumstances we will experience based on the thoughts and feelings we're having. This is how the manifestation process works. It's really quite simple. We can look at the financial breakdowns, which are at the source of our darkness and disempowerment, and now deny their power over us. We can no longer play dumb. What's wrong isn't outside of us. We have no control over what's 'out there.' Call upon the power of disciplined thoughts, emotions, spoken words, and imagination, and we can create abundance in every single corner of life. These magic wands came as standard equipment at birth, but the operator's manual has been missing. Until now.

There is within us vast innate knowledge, but our true heritage has been hidden. We are all angels clumsily making our way through this very human experience. We've been living within the ordinary world that is completely non-magical, but our abilities are inborn. It is only when we clear the debris of our humanness that we are free to become the powerhouses we were born to be.

Our guardian angels are always beside us, guiding us every step of the way, and they call upon us to seek the sky together. They hear our mental requests for assistance, so we must quiet the inner noise in order to hear their direction. We can create from what the darkness has already destroyed, but we must turn our attention inward to midwife the miraculous that awaits us. We were created by God, and if we allow the mystical and profound light to burst forth into our human experience, darkness shall be no more. We're drunk on something, and it's called infinite possibility. To create a future very much unlike the past, we linger no more over how small we were playing at life. As we emerge from the shadows of our suffering, we are made new.

Your life is a creation of your own, and it's about time you started living it out loud. You're in wizard training, and the more you learn to harness the miraculous power within, the further your wings will reach. Your powerful magic wands must be garlanded together with the thread of intentionality, as intentionality is requisite to mastering these creative tools. Each day, you'll be practicing the mastery of your powerful magic wands to deliberately create your every experience in life. Mark my words: the best is yet to come. Material abundance shall erupt.

It is time to experience the abundance that lies within you. You were born with enormously creative powers, and mastering that power grants you access to creating physical reality out of thin air. No longer are you numb to your greatness, and it won't serve you to play it any differently from this day forward. This book is a reminder for souls. Embrace the divine that is within. Today marks the beginning of your new life. You're rebranding yourself. You are the most adored creature. You are so blessed. You are so loved. How could you not be? You were created by the most epic force of love imaginable.

I was born out of an unimaginable depth of great love. I am pure love.

I am the creative mind of God.

> "It is not God's function to create or uncreate the circumstances or conditions of your life. God created you in the image and likeness of God. You have created the rest, through the power God has given you. God created the process of life and life itself as you know it. Yet God gave you free choice, to do with life as you will."
> **-Neale Donald Walsch**

There is great power within me. I am powerful beyond measure.

TODAY'S GOALS

Do not dwell on the future, nor the past, but in the NOW. Live each day as if it is your last. If you should leave this world today, what would be unfinished in your life? Record that here, and today begin the completion of it.

- My children's raising
- Octavis last unit
- Estate planning
- goals unreached
- not fit/strong

> "Everyone who is seriously involved in the pursuit of science becomes convinced that a spirit is manifest in the laws of the Universe — a spirit vastly superior to that of man... In this way the pursuit of science leads to a religious feeling of a special sort, which is indeed quite different from the religiosity of someone more naive."
> **-Albert Einstein**

THINGS FOR WHICH I'M GRATEFUL

Start viewing pain, disappointments, and challenges as opportunities for your spiritual growth. These are simply opportunities for self-mastery. Whatever it is you're going through, you'll get through it. Having a bad day? You'll get through it. The car broke down? You'll get through it. Going through bankruptcy? You'll get through it? During times such as these, remember what Winston Churchill said, "If you're going through hell, keep going."

So many dreams of yours are now in midst of coming true.

> "Don't look further for answers: be the solution. You were born with everything you need to know. Make a promise to stop getting in the way of the blessing that you are. Take a deep breath, remember to have fun, and begin."
> **-Jonathan H. Ellerby**

Day 4- The Mortal Mind: Our Command Center

"You create continually with your thoughts. You can create basically the same life with very little difference over and over again, year after year. You can experience the same life relentlessly, with a little different color to it, a slightly altered texture. Or you can co-create with God, moving confidently in the direction of your dreams." -Mary Manin Morrissey

Why are you always broke? Why is it that you experience the same financial breakdowns over and over again? You may yearn for a new career, yet you continue only to find the same job again and again. Brace yourself. I have news for you. You are creating all of this.

We've unknowingly become the authors of our own misfortunes. We've become so conditioned to our daily lives and the way in which we create and go about our daily lives that we actually believe that we have no control at all. And the cycle certainly does seem endless. Just as we recover from one financial meltdown, the next one begins. We live at survival level, so taking on a new positive attitude seems futile when we're up to our necks in overwhelm of the money breakdowns. Talk about insanity. Read it, but please don't weep, Oh, self-defeating, negative pain-in-the-keister that you are at times. You are not cursed. No, no, no. In plain terms, you've fallen victim to S.S.D.D.: Same Shitski, Different Day.

We create constantly, and the fact of the matter is that we've been creating our own reality all along, and we've been doing so by default. Despite our best efforts and no matter how well-intentioned we are, there's a pattern that's present- a brain pattern, and it's causing all the breakdowns around our finances. All along, we've been at the mercy of the mortal mind, and unbeknownst to us, it's been running the show, which is precisely why we experience S.S.D.D. with our finances. In order to create big miracles, we'll need to understand how the mortal mind operates and how this dysfunctional brain pattern came to be.

Everything that occurs in our finances is always colored by the experiences and the emotional responses we've had to the financial experiences in our past. The human brain is marvelous and wildly complex. Our brains remember and store every thought, feeling, image, and experience we've ever had, and the brain develops patterns based on our similar life experiences. These patterns create our dominant programming, and our dominant programming is what creates and attracts all of our life experiences (S.S.D.D.). When we have a negative thought about money and we focus some attention on the thought, the thought becomes more dominant and more potent. By directing more of our attention to the negative money thought, we create more thoughts that are similar to the original thought and a negative emotional response is generated. We continue with these repeated negative money thought forms and their emotional reactions that a dominant negative money brain pattern develops, and this brain pattern automatically sends the same thoughts and emotional responses from our past money experiences to our current money experiences. It is the repeated responses from the negative money brain pattern that molds our financial reality and perpetuates S.S.D.D..

95% of our reactions to life originate from our subconscious, from the beliefs and perceptions that created our brain patterns to begin with. The brain is always responding to current circumstances with past-based stored memories, and the brain does not know the difference between what it currently sees in its environment and what it remembers. This is precisely why we see repeated financial breakdowns. The brain will always respond with the conditioned pattern associated with a similar past experience. If financial havoc is a constant, we can consider the brain pattern from which we've been operating.

I won't give you any rah-rah bull-hockey nonsense. It's going to take effort to create a new brain pattern that fosters prosperity, but I assure you the outcome is clever, crisp and beautifully cosmo. Your financial transformation requires deliberate mental monitoring. There is no other way. It entails the constant monitoring and managing of your thoughts, emotions, spoken words, and imagination. The past has programmed you. In order to lay down new programming, daily and intentional practice for a period of time is required.

There are no victims in life, only creators. Which do you choose to be? You have created your life exactly as it is. Every thought, every word, every feeling, every imagining is pure creative energy. You've created a reality around money that has kept money away from you. It's time to create something new. Whatever is possible in the mind is possible in reality. The power to create is something we're all born with, and what you create is completely up to you. Your soul is calling you to do so. You have more power than you've given yourself credit for. Allow this book to steady the course and keep you on track. You're creating with purpose and using your magic wands with sublime intention. There's abundance in the wind, and with it is an ocean of cosmic blessings. Prepare for it.

I now monitor my every thought to be certain they're creating a future I want.

TODAY'S GOALS

If you ask me, it's far better to live each day with crystal clear goals, feeling fully alive instead of in a dull fog. You're training your brain to concentrate well. Goals provide the access to taming your fast moving thoughts. No longer do you sit around thinking about what you want to accomplish. No, no, no. You're taking effective actions to produce real results. Tally Ho!

THINGS FOR WHICH I'M GRATEFUL
Bold, beautiful new worlds are now gently tumbling into existence for me.

Day 5 - 'In the Beginning...': The Gospel of Prosperity

"The experience of life that you're creating is largely determined by your beliefs and attitudes. Your beliefs and attitudes are enormously powerful in the life you're living. Not only do these beliefs and attitudes continue to determine your inner experience of life, but they are also creative blueprints. They are blueprints, through which and by which a power greater than you, creates the outer events in your experience and tendencies in your life path. We call this power the law of mind or the creative mind principle." -Dr. Roger Teel

Brace yourself. You'll be doing some excavating today in a place invisible to everyone's eyes, including your own. At the onset of Peter Gabriel's 1992 music video "Digging in the Dirt," the word "DIG" takes shape in the grass, as murky, dark, and disturbing imagery overtakes the scene. Dense, overrun foliage consumes Gabriel as he is buried alive. He morphs into a skeleton in his struggle to excavate himself from his own grave. In the end, a twinkle of hope emerges as the word "HELP" appears, transforming into the word "HEAL" as Gabriel symbolically ascends from the dirt clad all in white. I know what you're going through. I've been there. Living a life steeped in financial havoc can be overwhelmingly suffocating, especially when your desperate, silent screams for "Help!" are falling on deaf ears. Take heart. The cavalry of hope has arrived, darling. You're in good hands. Your healing begins today.

When the eyes are shut, the light cannot be seen. To those who look inward, the key to the kingdom awaits. Today, you'll begin digging in your own dirt until you reach the source of the programming you have in place that keeps you stuck in your current financial situation. This programming—your core beliefs—are what's really running the show.

So what does money *really* mean to you? The thoughts and beliefs you have regarding money have remained in a dark, looming shadow for so long that once you consciously bring them into the light and simply acknowledge the darkness, shame, and fear that you've created around money, the transformation of the negative reprogramming you've had in place for decades can finally occur.

Like many of us, I'd been programmed with my own negative opinions of the wealthy as validation for my own lack of easily acquired affluence. We feel anger and resentment that we don't have money. We feel guilty for wanting money, and we feel guilty for having money when we see someone who has none. We grapple with the thought of being a good person who craves financial success. We can block the flow of money into our life by thinking we don't deserve it or by feeling guilty for wanting more of it. Renouncing money in favor of God has been the directive of many spiritual foundations throughout the history of mankind. We seem to have confused the warning against worshipping money with the ability to utilize money as a resource.

No one was intended to be poor. We've either thought of money as a sign of God's blessing, or as ruling supremely against the idea of being spiritually connected to God or religion. We have set up a battlefield between our spiritual beliefs and our earthly wants. We're the ones who attach guilt to money not God. God loves us and wants us to experience profound joy and love. If money provides the experience of that, God doesn't mind it one bit.

You may feel lost and alone in a financial no-man's land. But today is the day you'll get to the heart of the matter: the source of your suffering. You'll want to discover the core beliefs you have regarding money to reveal what it is that you really tell yourself is true about wealth, your source of income, money, and the bills that arrive in the mail. This is the incessant chatter, the inner-thought dialogue that runs on auto-pilot in your head. Some of your negative money beliefs might be:

I don't deserve to have money.
I never have enough money.
Money is evil.
Money causes corruption.
I am poor.
I'm barely able to pay my bills.
I live paycheck to paycheck.
I'm a financial failure.
I'm a loser.
Money doesn't grow on trees.
Rich people are dishonest.
I am always in debt.
My parents were poor, and I will be poor.
I just want someone else to take care of me.
The bills just keep coming in.
It's just so hard to survive these days.
Without a college degree, I can't make a lot of money.

Money is filthy and dirty.
Another financial Depression is coming.
The economy is so bad, I can barely survive.
Money only comes from hard work.
We're in a recession, so everyone is broke.
I resent others who have money.
Everything is so expensive nowadays.
I can't afford nice things.
The economy is bad, so I won't be able to make more money.
I'm always broke.
I am the unluckiest person I know.
I can't afford to do anything.
Life is hard.
Money always goes out faster than it comes in.
I don't deserve anything good to happen for me.
The unemployment rate is so high, there's no way I can get another job.

How many of these beliefs do you hold? They are the cause of your every financial breakdown, and they've been running the show all along. Whether you're aware of it or not, your ideas about success, your worthiness of it, how it can be achieved and how capable you are to create it have been acquired from the opinion of others. You've been strapped with negative money conversations. Perhaps they're what your family believed about money and you decided somewhere along the way that this was true for you as well. These beliefs can travel from generation to generation in families. But knowing where they came from isn't as important as realizing that you adopted the money beliefs of others and made them your own. You formed thoughts around them, and thoughts create.

I grew up in a household where the conversation around money was heavily steeped in fiscal lack and struggle. My parents grew up on the south side of Chicago born during a time when millions were out of work. They were products of the Great Depression, one of the worst economic slumps in our country. They became far too familiar with financial devastation. It was a time when everyone made do with what they had. My grandparents patched their children's clothes, as there was no money to buy new clothes. They went without food because there was none. They avoided banks because they didn't trust them. The Depression's legacy left an indelible mark on my parents' ability to believe that abundance could easily be theirs.

We stumble as parents and as a result we unintentionally hold back our very own children. The Depression brought years of chafing for my parents under the oppressive weight of a financial cancer that eventually metastasized to their beloved children. Their money beliefs were shaped by their experiences during the epoch of financial drought in which they grew up. I inherited the legacy of a faulty financial belief system from the generations before me, but by some miracle I was plucked out of the pile and graced with small mercies along the way that radically altered my life. Thank you, God.

We want abundance, but the fact is, very few of us have the mindset necessary to attract great wealth. Beliefs about money have become the dominant programming in your mind that has led you down a path of quiet desperation or resignation. Where these beliefs originated does not matter. No one is to blame.

Let's take a peek at the belief system that keeps you stymied, shall we? Allow yourself to get quiet and go within. Take several deep breaths and slowly exhale each time. Relax. Once you're completely relaxed, give permission and allow in all the ideas and beliefs you have about money. What is it that you say to yourself consciously or unconsciously about money? Record these thoughts below:

_____
_____
_____
_____
_____
_____
_____
_____
_____
_____
_____
_____

Reader, meet your brain patterns. Whatever your financial circumstances are, *you created them all,* and you created them with a faulty belief system that formed the unworkable brain patterns. Like it or not, you are that powerful. These are your money stories, the thoughts you have in your head and the conversations you have with others regarding money. We are so eager and willing to share with others all the things that aren't working well in our lives, our finances included. No wonder we struggle. Your thoughts are creative, and your words produce the thought into being. Both have given birth to the reality you're experiencing right now. This thorny landscape of negative programming is precisely what blocks your intriguing new life of prosperity. You've been hard-wired with these brain patterns, and only you can order a rewire.

Notice when the negative programming kicks in. It's the inner chatter, the habitual quiet dialog that goes on in your head whenever the subject of money comes up. As you begin to practice a new habit of thought, your old, limiting patterns of thought that have kept you wrenched and wrung out over financial strife will begin to shift. The process of taking conscious control of your own life has begun, and the creation of any income you desire is imminent. Do everything this book says and you'll make an earth-shattering shift in your finances. This may not be easy for you at first. In fact, it could be a bit confronting, and you may want to stop doing the exercises in this book. That's okay. When you're ready to move forward again, you will. For years, perhaps even decades, you've been buying into a negative financial belief system that has not served you; otherwise money wouldn't be a concern.

Allow yourself to let go with wild abandon. Let go of the guilt. Let go of your feelings of scarcity. Ours is a land of abundant opportunity for everyone. Know that there is more than enough to go around for each and every one of us. Release the feeling of not being good enough, smart enough, whatever enough. Enough is enough. Those thoughts have been self-defeating, belittling, and they undercut your cosmic capabilities. True prosperity begins with feeling good about yourself and being happy no matter what. It is a state of mind. This is an especially big deal, and you're going to learn why.

Rest assured that just around the corner, in the unseen mist, astonishing treasures and spellbinding coincidences are emerging that you can't even imagine. You're developing an entirely new conversation about money, and you can get to whatever financial circumstance you want from wherever you are, right here, right now. This change may be a gradual one, depending on how ingrained your negative thoughts about money are, or you may be able to make a quantum leap quickly if you embrace the ideas and concepts in this book and apply them diligently each day. Now that you're aware of what lurks beneath the surface and keeps abundance at bay, you'll begin to integrate new programming into your brain on a daily basis to powerfully attract all the goodness that is your birthright.

The many ways you've been negative with your thoughts and conversations have blocked your shining magnificence, invalidating who you really are. There will be no more living at half throttle. Those days are over. Monetary demons can no longer crucify you. You are so fortunate to have a shot at this. Your parents and grandparents most likely did not. From this day forward, nothing can throw you off course. Nothing. The murky spell that had been cast is lifting. Your sacred nature is emerging. Keep your eyes on the sky. Miracles are everywhere. You're on the cusp of a richer, better, and deeper life. Prepare to claim it.

My income is constantly increasing.

> "Our way of thinking creates good or bad outcomes."
> **-Stephen Richards**

> "In your hands will be placed the exact results of your thoughts; you will receive that which you earn, no more, no less. Whatever your present environment may be, you will fail, remain, or rise with your thoughts, your wisdom, desire, as great as your dominant aspiration."
> **-James Allen**

TODAY'S GOALS
Everything I touch turns to gold.

There are no throwaway moments. And every, single day matters. Without actions, there are no results. Get rid of anything that isn't useful, beautiful or doesn't bring you joy. Separate these items into 3 boxes: garbage, donate, and sell. You're redesigning your life to look exactly the way you want it to be. Begin with your home. By cleaning out the clutter in your surroundings, you clear the clutter in your mind.

_____   _____
_____   _____
_____   _____
_____   _____

> "The universe is change; our life is what our thoughts make it."
> **-Marcus Aurelius**

THINGS FOR WHICH I'M GRATEFUL
Dare to dream. Dare to reach for the stars. Dare to claim all that is your birthright.

_____   _____
_____   _____
_____   _____

Something deep inside of you remembers exactly what it's like to be fearless.

Day 6 - The Blueprint of Your New Intriguing Life

"You cannot change your destination overnight, but you can change your direction overnight." -Jim Rohn

Volte-face is a French term that means a reversal in policy or opinion; an about-face. My dear friend, you've begun your very own financial *volte-face*, and as a result, you're giving birth to a profound inner shift that is changing the direction of your life. You are destined for your own brand of greatness. Can you feel it? There is great abundance within us all. It's always been there for the asking. When you conjure up a wish with a wand, you do so with precision. You can have whatever you want in life. All that is needed to bring it into existence is determination, focus, and a vivid picture of what you desire. It's time to turn on your passion.

A Vision Board is a clear visual representation, a collage of the things that you want to have, be, or do in life. There is real power in this tool, so employ it. The right side of the brain is where our feelings and our creativity are generated. This portion of the brain responds to images and the feelings associated with those images. The right side of the brain cannot distinguish the difference between what is imagined and what is real. Plying the power of your vastly creative imagination will reproduce in reality the images and words on your Vision Board. You'll be creating your own Vision Board with images and words that depict all the wonderful things you want to create in your life. By selecting images that appeal to your emotions (feelings of pure excitement, happiness, unbridled joy and passion), you give birth to their creation.

Manifesting is our birthright. Whatever is possible in the mind is possible in reality. Before something can manifest in your life, you must first clearly imagine it. I've been using Vision Boards for years. By becoming quite proficient at using all of the tools outlined in this book, my income had substantially increased, and I was ready to upgrade my house. As my realtor, Debi, began showing me house after house, I grew frustrated that none of them were what I liked. I realized I was struggling to find my new home because I didn't have a precise picture in my head of what I wanted this new home to look like. So I began searching through magazines until I found a house I adored, and I posted the picture of it on my refrigerator. Each time I'd look at the picture, I'd close my eyes and imagine myself living in that house, relaxing in the fragrant gardens, and having friends over for dinner. I completely enjoyed fantasizing about that new house of mine. It felt good, almost euphoric, so I imagined it frequently.

One Friday afternoon, I took a drive through one of the more desirable neighborhoods I wanted to live. I noticed a beautiful Italian-style brick home with lots of great architectural detail. I pulled the car over to the curb and studied the house, wondering who the lucky soul was that lived in such a beautiful place. The next day, I drove by that same house again, only now there was a 'For Sale' sign in the yard. The universe is funny, I thought to myself. I immediately called Debi and asked her to get all the details on this place. I knew I had to have this house. Debi gave me all the details and then provided me with the asking price. It was $100,000 more than what I wanted to pay, but we scheduled an appointment anyway to tour the place that night. It was love at first sight. The house had incredible crown molding, arched doorways, hardwood floors, three fireplaces, and every bedroom had its own unique and beautiful bathroom. Debi submitted my offer of $100,000 less than the asking price, and though the house had been on the market less than 24 hours, my offer was accepted within three hours. I had been so caught up in the excitement of how easily and effortlessly this process had turned out for me, it wasn't until months later that I unpacked a box that had the picture I'd kept on my refrigerator: I was now living in a house that was a close replica of the style of the house in that picture. Amazing, isn't it? I'd been led to that house. Divinely guided, actually. That's the magic of this exquisite mind work.

HOW TO MAKE AND USE YOUR VISION BOARD

Supplies Needed:
- Poster Board
- Large Assortment of Magazines
- Glue or Rubber Cement
- Scissors

Begin today by paging through magazines and selecting pictures that clearly illustrate what you want your life to look like. Choose images that resonate from your heart and make you feel giddy with anticipation. If your goal is to have a six figure income, then select pictures of a lifestyle congruent with that six figure income. Ask yourself these questions:

- *Where would you live?*
- *What do you want your surroundings to look like?*
- *What kind of car would you drive?*
- *Where would you travel?*
- *What things would you own?*
- *What do you physically want to look like? What would you wear? What does your body look like?*
- *What kind of job would you have?*

Complete your Vision Board within the next few days and place it in a location that gives you as much visual exposure to it as possible throughout the day. I keep mine in my bathroom. I place my undivided attention on each image as I brush my teeth morning and night. Place yours wherever you'll see it frequently throughout the day and intentionally focus on the images.

It's far better to live each day with a crystal clear vision of what you want in life, so get your vision board complete within the next few days. This is your visual display of cosmic blessing, so gaze at it often. I do not know the date I will die, but the way in which I approached this work is what now defines me and my legacy. It will be the same for you.

Take a gander at what's on the horizon. The house, the car, the career, and the lifestyle that have simply been distant and blurry desires are now beginning to materialize. Excitement is now your current state-of-mind. Anything you can imagine you have already earned. Get whimsical, you powerful gladiator, you, and begin the decoration of your beautiful new life.

This is the most stunning year of my life.

I see my new life of prosperity clearly, and I focus on this vision frequently.

Something wonderful is happening to me today--I can feel it.

> "I am the greatest."
> **-Mohammad Ali**

> "You have powers you never dreamed of. You can do things you never thought you could do. There are no limitations in what you can do except the limitations of your own mind."
> **-Darwin P. Kingsley**

All my wishes CAN come true, and I'm making this happen right here, right now.

TODAY'S GOALS

You will never get up the mountain by wishing yourself to the top. No, no, no. You must climb. This work is about utilizing the gifts and talents you've been given—to know what being alive really means. Life is wonderful; life is exhilarating; and life is bringing the rewards and opportunities you've always dreamed of so get excited. Golden opportunities are on your horizon. Get started on your Vision Board, so your new life begins to materialize.

_____   _____
_____   _____
_____   _____
_____   _____

THINGS FOR WHICH I'M GRATEFUL
Go now and amaze yourself!

_____   _____
_____   _____
_____   _____

> We work on ourselves inconsistently, which is why we spin out of control on a regular basis. You've made a lifestyle decision here, haven't you? You're putting in place new architecture that will radically alter your life in ways you only dreamed of until now. In order to keep your possibility of financial freedom alive and growing, read this book each morning before you begin the day, and you will usher in unexplained occurrences that magically draw to you everything you need with little or no effort. Intentionally end your day peacefully. Should you choose to expand who you are with this work, you'll be met with miraculous power bound by nothing.

Day 7 - Ordinary or Extraordinary: Which do you choose to be?

"Ordinary people believe only in the possible. Extraordinary people visualize not what is possible or probable, but rather what is impossible. And by visualizing the impossible, they begin to see it as possible." -Cherie Carter-Scott

Financial lack is an equal opportunity oppressor. There is no vein of misery that runs deeper in all our lives than that of not having enough money to easily pay our bills. My fear of poverty knew exactly where to tighten the screws on my soul. Frustration, anger, and panic had become familiar companions. My life felt ordinary, and I was beginning to believe my ship had passed with so many clandestine dreams of mine gone awry. As we headed to divorce court, I was crumbling under an all-consuming fear of an unknown future. I'd become the worst version of myself, lashing out at Frank and blaming him for the palpable discontent that was governing my everyday life. I could see no way of generating enough money to sustain me and my two boys, and the angst and drama of it all made me restless, sleepless, and listless.

One day, I was weeding through some boxes in the basement when I opened a box filled with books I'd read in my twenties. *Living in the Light* and *Creative Visualization* were the first titles I pulled from the box. Both books were written by Shakti Gawain, a leader in the world consciousness movement. Her books introduced me to a whole new way of thought that I found so fascinating that I devoured scores of similar books on positive thought, creative thought, and the manifestation process. But insight is useless unless it is practiced. Before me were the books I'd read a decade earlier but did nothing with the content. I unpacked several of them and brought them upstairs and for the next month I began to re-read them. Only this time I took notes. Soon I was practicing the mind power techniques outlined on the pages. The darkness of my emotions slowly began to subside as the sun began breaking through the clouds. I could finally see the sky again and substantial peace began to emerge. All along I thought I had outer worlds to conquer, but my inner world was where I found my real power, my real sustenance.

It wasn't long before I embarked on an all-out prosperity rampage. I made the reprogramming of my mind my full-time job, and I didn't miss a day of work. I created a disciplined routine that I followed without fail at set times throughout the day. I was taking creative control of my own mind, so it worked for me and with me—not against me as it had done most of my entire adult life—and my sacred adventure blossomed. Were it not for this work, I would have forever lost contact with my soul.

Think about what it would be like having an all-powerful magic genie at your disposal who asks you to make an unlimited number of wishes. What would your wishes be? The only limitations are those you've established in your own mind or have permitted others to set for you. Allow the sky to be the limit today and make a list of the desires you carry in your heart. What is it you want? A new car, a new house, a new job, a promotion in your current job, a hefty savings account, a new wardrobe, a vacation? Jot down all the things you dream about having and the things you'd like to do. Use the next page to continue writing down your wish list.

_____
_____
_____

_____

_____

_____

_____

_____

_____

_____

_____

Notice the thoughts you had as you made your wish list. Were they thoughts that made you excited or doubtful? Just notice them and see where your mind drifts. Now determine the income you'd like to generate in the next year. (Please be generous with yourself.) Absolutely anything is possible for you. It isn't about how much you *think* you can earn but how much you *desire* to create and receive.

Record the amount of money you are requesting from the Universe here:

$ _____

The income amount you just requested will be the primary financial goal you'll be concentrating on for the next several weeks. Write this income amount on note cards and place the note cards in areas where you'll see them often. Also write this dollar figure on the center of your Vision Board. You can achieve whatever you can see in your mind, so dream without limits, you illustrious angel, you. Nothing has ever been wrong with you. Your mind is holy, but you'd forgotten that. Allow divinity to pull you to a higher ground and embrace the enchanting soul within. You're equipped with something you haven't known how to access. Admit you have incredible power and begin the practice of it. It exists to be used by you, and not using it is the same as having no power at all.

Once you expand your head, there is no shrinking back to who you once were. For the remainder of the day, place your attention often on the amount of money you just requested on the previous page. The direction of your life is about to change. I can assure you that once you begin practicing the principles outlined in this manual, your income will begin to increase. You are no different than me. Money shall soon become a long-overdue concern of the past. Unabashed joy will be wildly unleashed into your daily experience, and you will be unrecognizable. Oh my stars! You're burning the candle not only at both ends, but in the middle. You're just getting warmed up. Have a nice day.

I ask and I am always given.

> "Whatever we think becomes sooner or later translated into action; and as upon our actions our life depends, it will be seen that it is possible by thought control to govern our life. For by controlling our thoughts we govern our actions; by governing our actions we mould our life and circumstances, thus shaping our fate."
> **-Henry Thomas Hamblin**

I now easily and effortlessly earn over $_____**each year.**

TODAY'S GOALS

The champion is strong within you. When you raise the bar, you jump higher. Just how high will you jump today? Jot down your goals for today and complete on all of them.

_____ _____
_____ _____
_____ _____
_____ _____

> "People with goals succeed because they know where they are going. It's as simple as that."
> **-Earl Nightingale**

THINGS FOR WHICH I'M GRATEFUL

You create and manifest everything you want and need through focused intention.

_____ _____
_____ _____
_____ _____

Money always flows easily and effortlessly to me.

I am always at the right place at the right time.

Day 8 - Affirmations: Say it is so, and it is.

"As a single footstep will not make a path on the earth, so a single thought will not make a pathway in the mind. To make a deep physical path, we walk again and again. To make a deep mental path, we must think over and over the kind of thoughts we wish to dominate our lives." -Henry David Thoreau

We've been at the mercy of a frantic mind, and it's been running the show. Our agitated and fearful thoughts create a very agitated and fear-filled reality. Our relentless foul moods are so exhausting they wear us to a nub. Our emotions can be a heavy burden to bear. There's always a high personal price to pay when we falter in darkness and simmer in negativity. It is here that emotional danger looms. Until we shift our thoughts, we cannot break the cycle.

The repetition of a particular thought is a zenith manifestation tool that attracts that on which we are focusing. The brain learns through repetition and concentration. Our most primary skills—language, reading, math, walking—were all learned through repetition and concentration. When you repeatedly concentrate on a particular thought, you radically increase its strength and create more of the same kinds of thoughts that cluster together and interconnect in the brain. The more thoughts you think in kind carve a deeper mental pathway. An affirmation is the repetition of an intentional thought, a concentrated and specific declaration that something is so. By affirming, you are declaring exactly what it is that will occur for you. Infinite intentions are set through affirmations.

Every moment of every day, we are always in the process of creating. What occurs in the mind creates what occurs outside of us. Thoughts have creative power, and if a thought is strong enough, it will manifest. Never, ever underestimate the potency of affirmations in the manifestation process. They are the pathway to abundance. By repeatedly affirming something, you make a request for the creation of it. The mind hears it and repeats more of the same, and a new pathway of thought now begins in the brain. By affirming the thought over and over again, your brain becomes conditioned to believing it's true. Frequent and focused repetition of the same thought causes the brain to firmly remember it, and it then becomes the dominant way of thought. Repeat a new thought often enough with enough positive conviction, and a new brain pattern is formed.

For an affirmation to create prosperity in your life, it must be very specific, in the present tense, repeated often, and usually begins with "I am" or "I now". For example, if you'd like to find a new higher-paying job, an effective affirmation to manifest that job would be, *"I now easily and effortlessly find the perfect job that pays me more than (insert amount of money you'd like to make)."* Since you no longer choose to struggle with money issues, including the words "easily and effortlessly" in an affirmation will create the result with ease and little effort. Also, you don't want to limit the good that will come to you, so include the words "more than" whenever you're affirming a specific income amount. Get the picture? Remember, whatever you repeatedly think and speak about money will occur so be intentional about every word you choose for your affirmations. In saying so, you make it so.

Today, you'll create the affirmations that reflect the financial outcome you desire. That which you repeatedly affirm will always occur in reality, so be precise with the wording of them.

Keep your affirmations in the present tense *as if the situation is already happening.* Affirming *"I want to earn $100,000 a year"* will only keep you *wanting* a larger income. Repeatedly saying *"With a lot of work I will be attracting money"* will assure that you attract money only if you work hard. Since you want to create abundance easily and quickly, this affirmation is far more potent: *"I now earn over $100,000 each year easily and effortlessly."*

Focusing the power of thought for the specific purpose of creating the things you want in your life is what affirmations are all about. What you put your attention on grows. By focusing the energies of your mind on the things you want to have, you cause them into reality. Affirmations gave rise to the genesis of my financial transformation. During my quest for prosperity, I plastered scores of note cards with affirmations everywhere in my house. I'm sure my children thought I'd lost any sanity that remained. What they didn't know was that I'd stumbled on the colossal power of my mind, and I was directing it to attract the life I'd always hoped for. I was getting excited, and it felt good. Really, really good. Destiny was calling, and it was on loudspeaker. I knew as sure as the sky was blue that I would get exactly what I was affirming and more. It was simply a matter of time, so I began doing more of it. I began taking daily 20-minute walks where I'd parrot my affirmations over and over in my head, and within a short period of time, my life that seemed so out of kilter now felt sanctified. I was being pulled out of the emotional plunge. I could feel it.

Action:

Call to mind the income amount you created on paper yesterday and create an affirmation to repeat on a daily basis. *Remember, affirmations must be specific, positive, and in the present tense.* Here's the affirmation I used years ago when I started with this process: *"I now easily and effortlessly earn over $100,000 each year at a job that I love with a flexible schedule and great insurance benefits."*

Now it's your turn. Create your new income affirmation below:

_____

Your second affirmation will be another money declaration. You'll want to create one that makes you feel good, or you can use one from the list below.

- *Money comes to me easily and effortlessly.*
- *I am always at the right place at the right time.*
- *I now live in a beautiful house that I easily afford.*
- *Divine Guidance is my only reality, and Divine Guidance richly manifests constant prosperity in my life.*
- *I am a divine magnet for prosperity.*
- *I am always lucky.*
- *Everything I touch is a success.*
- *I am a magnet for Divine prosperity.*
- *Riches of every sort are drawn to me.*

- *Golden Opportunities are everywhere for me.*
- *I am financially blessed beyond my wildest dreams.*
- *There are always plenty of customers for my services.*

You get the idea. Create an affirmation that states *exactly* what it is that you want to occur for you and write your second affirmation here:

_____

This next concept is an important one: *Do not get caught up in worrying about or figuring out "how" this will happen.* I repeat: *Do not get caught up in worrying about or figuring out "how" this will happen.* You have all the cosmic support you need. Angels are guiding you every step of the way. The only requirement is to generate from within using your magic wands of thought, emotion, spoken words, and imagination. Golden opportunities will become obvious to you, and prosperity will begin appearing in all sorts of ways that you simply won't believe it. Believe it. It's a sign that the process is taking hold. Prosperity has marked you as an easy target. You may find money on the sidewalk or in the pocket of an old coat pocket that you haven't worn for years. You may be offered something for free. However it begins to show up for you, notice that you're causing the shift in your consciousness to occur and make note of it all.

Allow providence to intervene on your behalf. Enchantment patiently awaits you. Can you dig it?? Today begin to repeat and fully concentrate on your affirmations. This is priceless instruction, so follow it. Get yourself several notebooks and keep them handy to write your affirmations several times throughout the day and before you go to sleep at night. You'll also write them in this book. Writing them 10-20 times in the morning is a great way to begin your day. Write them while you wait at the doctor's office, or as you wait in the car for the kids. You may notice that when you're repeatedly writing the same affirmations your mind may drift to other matters. That's okay. Notice that even when thinking about other things, you're still able to write your affirmations. *Your mind is always listening and paying attention, so feed it only what you want to grow.*

Write your affirmations on plain or colored note cards and place them in areas where you'll see them often, such as the bathroom mirror, near the kitchen sink, in your car, near your computer, in your wallet, on the walls in your home and workplace. Every time you see the note card, you'll trigger a reminder to repeat the affirmation.

You're staring at golden heights, wondering if you're ready for the climb. Believe me. You're ready. There's a remarkable feeling of life surging all around you- the feeling of excitement and awe from giving it your all. Shine on, you crazy diamond. Ready or not, here you come.

I create constantly with my thoughts. Thought is cause. Experience is effect.

I now easily and effortlessly earn over $_____**each year.**

TODAY'S GOALS

With training, you will automatically think the thoughts and speak the words that produce abundance in your life, and you will be met with miracles at every turn.
Concentrate well and concentrate often today.

_____   _____
_____   _____
_____   _____
_____   _____

THINGS FOR WHICH I'M GRATEFUL

Be grateful for every, single wonderful quality you possess, and there are many. Let your focus shift. You are dazzling. You're taking the world by storm. Success is yours.
You are a magnet for all that is good.

_____   _____
_____   _____
_____   _____

AFFIRMATIONS

Today begin the writing of your affirmations. Write them upon waking, just before you fall asleep at night, and as time allows throughout the day. Affirmations serve as the request for the prosperity you want in your life.

_____
_____
_____
_____
_____
_____
_____
_____
_____

Day 9 - Think and Grow Filthy Rich

"Thoughts are things. Thoughts create things. Thoughts shape things. Thoughts become ultimately, tangibly real." -Sir John Templeton

How do we sabotage ourselves? Let me count the ways. We lose our grip when our finances take a nose dive, yet we did not purposely cause this. This occurred by default from our unmanaged thoughts. Now we know better. Envy creeps in when we see others thriving around us. *When will our lucky break arrive?* We kill off our own success when we resent others for theirs. There is an infinite amount of abundance and prosperity out there for all of us. There is more than enough to go around for everyone. But the closer we are to having a breakthrough in our finances, the fiercer the struggle may seem. Cursed? No, far from it. All of your negative financial circumstances are a reflection of your own internal state, and absolutely no one can shield you from your own mind. Peace of mind is vital to your success. Take a deep breath. Very slowly breathe out. Relax. Be open. Be open to the multitude of new possibilities that await.

As we thinketh, so doeth we experience. It may take years for a particular thought or idea to appear in our lives, but it will appear eventually. It always does. Everything that occurs for you is in direct response to the thoughts you are thinking. If certain areas of your life are going well, the thoughts you have about that area in life are positive ones that cause you to be effective in those areas. Your finances aren't where you want them to be, so your thoughts about money are at the source of the breakdown. It all begins with a thought. Look around at what you have occurring in your finances right now and see what you've created in thought. Your life experiences are simply a mirror of the internal conversations taking place in your head. No matter what the financial shortfall is, these experiences are simply the outer effects of inner dialogue. You have been habitually thinking the same thought over and over and over, so it may not seem like you're choosing the thought, but you are.

The ability to use our minds to create what we want in our lives is the greatest gift from God. Whatever we put our attention on will eventually grow into being. A wand is a focused thought that jumpstarts the manifestation process. The wand of thought is cause. Experience is the effect—always. There is no financial circumstance so dire it cannot be changed by choosing higher thought forms. Whenever we consistently focus on a particular kind of thought, we give life to other thoughts that are similar, and the thoughts become even more powerful. A practiced thought becomes a dominant thought. We can engineer our every thought to grant us every wish we've ever wished.

You'll soon learn that when you declare and believe that everything always unfolds for you easily and effortlessly, you'll experience just that. Years ago, I bought an old Victorian house that, of course, I got at the perfect price. I'd been doing all the renovations myself which afforded me the perfect opportunity to repeat my affirmations hundreds (if not thousands) of times. The one I'd been focusing on was, *"I am always lucky."* I'd repeat this over and over and over as I scraped wallpaper and painted every room in that house. While I was installing shelving in my kitchen, my electric drill stopped working, so I told my boys I was heading to the hardware store to buy a new one. While I was driving, I noticed a bright yellow object in the middle of the road. Without giving it much thought, I pulled over, got out of my car and walked toward the object. As I got closer, I could see it was a relatively new Dewalt cordless drill that had apparently fallen off someone's truck. How lucky I was! I was giddy that I had easily, effortlessly, and quickly manifested a deluxe cordless drill far better than the electric one it would replace. You may be thinking coincidence played the starring role in my drill story, but there are no coincidences. Simply put, I attract good fortune on a regular basis because I say that I attract good fortune on a daily basis. *I am always lucky.*

You are either attracting money to you or repelling it from you. It's all based on how you think. It's not always easy to catch our negative thoughts because they move so quickly. We're fully engaged in thinking them, as they've become so ingrained in a habitual thought pattern. When we worry, anxious thoughts begin to overtake peace of mind. These fearful thoughts dart in all directions as if they're caught in a high-security prison searchlight trying to escape, and this devious gang is always up to no good. Whatever we're thinking about is creating our future, and worrying about money never makes it any easier to pay our bills. In fact, worrying about money (or the lack of it) deters, rather than attracts, prosperity. If you say that you think about money all the time, but you still don't have enough money to pay your bills, what you're really doing is worrying about money. It is here that fear and chaos rule. Worrying is very powerful creative energy, and it slays our potential. Correct your thinking, please.

Self-help guru, Louise Hay, has written scores of books on the power of the mind, and I've read nearly all of them. My mother is a professional worrier, and since she was a pivotal role model for me growing up, I was a worrying neophyte. When I was in the process of reinventing myself, I was in maximum worry overdrive. To counter this, I wrote one of Louise Hay's *Power Thoughts* on several post cards and placed it in areas I'd see it frequently. I repeated that affirmation incessantly: *"All is well. Everything is working out perfectly for my highest good. Out of this situation, only good will come. I am safe."* This worked miracles in my life, just as Louise Hay promised, and helped me shift from a state of panic and worry into one of peace of mind and contentment, with a sound belief that *all is well.*

If you don't control your thoughts, they will control you. Create a new thought edifice, and mentally fast to cleanse your inner dialogue of the thoughts that condemn your financial freedom. No one else thinks the thoughts in your head. There's no one else out there doing this for you. Begin to master your thoughts, and the direction of your life will change.

Disciplining your mind is not as challenging as it might seem. You *can* train your thoughts. Money affirmations create a new money brain pattern so repeatedly flood your mind with them. The brain loves patterns, so practice concentrating on abundance at the same times each day. You're being spurred to greater achievement, so intentionally choose what goes on in your head.

Sure, you may have been lost, but now you are found. Allow your thoughts to bless the world today. Very soon, these intentionally caused thoughts will shift to auto-pilot, and watercolor blue skies will be the norm for you. That's inevitable.

Your brain is becoming intoxicatingly bloated from all the new thoughts you're putting in there. You've glimpsed the beautiful new life that patiently waits, and it's yours for the taking. You're rebounding and dancing back into the light, so dust off your wings and put on your fancy dancing shoes. Cha Cha Cha.

And whenever there is a problem, repeat over and over: *"All is well. Everything is working out perfectly for my highest good. Out of this situation, only good will come. I am safe."*

It will create miracles in your life.

I now easily and effortlessly earn over $_____each year.

I dare to be great.

TODAY'S GOALS

Today is the day that absolutely everyone's dreams come true. Chica Boom!

THINGS FOR WHICH I'M GRATEFUL

I choose where I place my focus. I always focus on the positive in all situations.

AFFIRMATIONS

I am one wispy thought away from creating a beautiful new future for myself. If I hold onto that thought often enough that thought must manifest in my physical reality.

Day 10 - Planting New Seeds in the Fertile Garden of Your Mind

"Man's power of choice enables him to think like an angel or a devil, a king or a slave. Whatever he chooses, his mind will create and manifest." -Frederick Bailes

We've endured such a financially distressing year... again. Any sense of sanity has been destroyed by the trials and tribulations that never fail to keep us suffering. This road we walk on is not one we chose. No, it is not. We woke up one morning and discovered that ten years have passed us by, and we're still no further advanced than we were before. We keep waiting for the moment our lives will begin at last, but the moment has been patiently waiting all along for us to embrace it. We've been too distracted to notice. You simply need some buoying up. For goodness sake, tap into your God-given mind power and take control of your thoughts.

We know in our heart of hearts that we deserve something more out of life. We came to win. We came to thrive and to prosper. Let's just face it. We've been negative junkies. But there's a life force in us, and it's strong. We're in recovery, in remission, from the toxic, negative way of being we have had around money. Halleluiah. It's high time we dare to dream again. The antidote to what is out of whack in our finances is the cultivation of a lifestyle change in which we powerfully choose what we think about. We all have the power to turn darkness into light, and once we become intentional with our thoughts, we no longer remain an accident of circumstance.

If you persistently think a certain thought, it becomes part of both unconscious and deliberate action. By practicing concentration with deliberation, you train yourself to think so clearly, promptly, and decisively that you can manifest absolutely anything you desire, and you can do so quickly.

You can hope for financial transformation all you want, but this new life of yours is sourced in daily mental discipline. Affirmations allow the adoption of new beliefs. They form new brain patterns and allow the miracles you seek to unfold with little or no effort. To create a new money thought pattern, you must inundate the mind with your affirmations until they become the immediate and automatic thoughts you have about money. The more you repeat them, the faster your dreams take flight. It's the only way to reprogram the brain pattern that stymies your finances. Over time, you won't need to be so intentional, but if you want to have a rapid breakthrough in your finances, do this work like your life depends on it. The mind hears it all, and will begin to repeat more of the same kinds of thoughts... on its own... when you're not listening. This is how the mind operates. It's noisy and big, so you must develop the mental discipline to select your thoughts carefully.

Apply unwavering discipline to your mental endeavors and abundance will reverberate back to you like a boomerang. The change in your thought process gives birth to the big new life that's waiting for you to step into it. You are choosing to alter your thoughts, and by doing so you have the ability to alter any situation. When the negative thoughts begin to creep in, simply say, *"That's okay,"* and allow them to drift far, far away. 'That's okay' will be the trigger your mind needs to hear to release your attachment to the counterproductive thoughts. When you're being intentional with your thoughts, nothing can enter the inner sanctuary of the mind unless you allow it in.

Did you know that abundance is your natural state? Well, it is. By learning to focus your thinking, you set a new stage. Imagine the creative power of a thought repeated hundreds or even thousands of times. Thoughts with such repetition are extended outward for creation and will always be manifested. Always. Now do you see the benefit of repeating your affirmations?

If you believe you don't have the time to repeat your affirmations a hundred times daily just think about how many times each day you've unconsciously thought the negative thoughts that have held you back and kept you stagnant with money. Allow an intrusion into your busy schedule and dedicate time to your transformation.

It doesn't matter what you're doing or where you are. You can do this work anywhere and at any time. Repeat your affirmations while you're in the shower, driving the car, cutting the grass, mopping the floor, brushing your teeth, standing in line, changing a baby's diaper, or lying in bed. Clog dance around your living room as you sing them and allow yourself to feel like a kid again. My beautiful friend Linette dances while she sings her affirmations at night in her backyard, when it's dark and no one is looking, and she does so with wild abandon. Tape record 10-15 minutes of you speaking your affirmations and listen to them as you drift off to sleep at night. The point is: repeat, repeat, repeat! Immerse your mind with them, and you'll be forever changed at depth.

You're living life on purpose, and it's causing a cellular upheaval. Right here, right now, you are on the edge of what could be the greatest moment in your life, and it's too darn important to miss. You're flooding your subconscious with prosperous thoughts. It may seem as if you'll implode before the quantum leap forward takes place in your financial transformation. Don't stop now. Keep going. Your life *will* change.

It's an absolutely fabulous day, isn't it? Open your arms to the heavens and affirm the generosity of the cosmos. You are out on the other side of this soul's dark night. All there is to do is be still and remember who you are. You are called on to be bigger. There's a path being paved, so allow yourself to be guided down it. Filled with blessings and frolic, your new state of mind, this new mental perspective you've so boldly created, shall soon manifest.

Every day you get closer.

What if everything was always working out perfectly for me?

> "Our subconscious minds have no sense of humor, play no jokes and cannot tell the difference between reality and an imagined thought or image. What we continually think about eventually will manifest in our lives."
> **-Sidney Madwed**

> "The greatest force is derived from the power of thought. The finer the element, the more powerful it is. The silent power of thought influences people, even at a distance, because mind is one as well as many. The universe is a cobweb; minds are spiders."
> **-Swami Vivekananda**

I now easily and effortlessly earn over $_____each year.

TODAY'S GOALS

You are disciplined and always schedule the time to do the daily work to create abundance in your life. You deserve abundance. Abundance is your birthright. Simply train your mind to draw to you anything you want.

_____   _____
_____   _____
_____   _____
_____   _____

THINGS FOR WHICH I'M GRATEFUL

You have so very much to be grateful for. There is no one else like you. You are a living miracle. You are Divine magnificence- God's arms and legs on earth. Remember who you really are. That's how you access your power.

_____   _____
_____   _____
_____   _____

AFFIRMATIONS
I am the very best version of myself.

_____
_____
_____
_____
_____
_____
_____
_____
_____
_____
_____

Day 11- The Magic Wand of Emotions

"Where we invest our energy is a result of choice. No one outside of us forces us to invest our energy in any particular emotion, thought, or act. The energy investment choices we make are either conscious or unconscious. Either way, where we direct the energy of our thoughts and emotions gives rise to our experiences."–Michael Bernard Beckwith

You're thrillingly blessed with grit and fortitude. There is nothing you can't do. But sometimes your mood becomes so dark that you find yourself swimming against the tide once again. Fear not, sweet pea. Help is on the way. All the darkness in your life stems from the darkness in your mind. Victory lies in ascending above the mental forces that keep you stymied. You're no longer disillusioned once you begin to unravel the threads of your ethereal memory. A sacred fire smolders within, and once you understand profoundly who you are and what you're capable of creating, you will thrive and reach your greatest potential. You descended from heaven with a divine purpose of causing and experiencing unspeakable joy. This is your cosmic function. It's what you were born for. Only today, you're a little cranky.

We spend far too much time in emotional pain, and it's high time we stopped investing so much energy in such a dark place. We sorrow the soul when our mood sinks so low.

Thoughts are the first level in the creation process; emotions are the next level. Our emotions are not generated from the heart; they are generated in the mind. Our thoughts are what create our moods to begin with. They are kissing cousins. Every single thought we dwell on triggers a corresponding emotional response. Change your thoughts, and the emotions must follow suit.

Everything exists for joy, and how we feel is more important than anything else, especially when abundance is our target. There is astonishing power in our emotions, another one of our powerful magic wands. We came into this life fully prepared for this environment. Our emotions came as standard equipment at birth. *Absolutely nothing is more imperative than feeling good when you're working toward creating abundance.* Your state of mind and your emotions are the key drivers to getting more of anything quickly, both positive and negative.

You're creating every single second of the day, and your emotions are the built-in mechanism that indicates whether you're in a positive state of creation or a negative state of creation. All day long, you're feeling emotions, and your emotions can sanctify or poison.

There are positive emotions, and there are negative emotions. There is always a positive thought at the source of a positive emotion, and there is always a negative thought at the source of a negative emotion. Since our emotions serve as our very own personal navigation system, we can easily determine if we're creating something we desire or something we don't desire. We can actually *feel* our way in every moment to determine whether or not the thoughts we are thinking are creating prosperity or not. When our mood is negative, our emotions are signaling that we're headed away from prosperity. We powerfully create prosperity in every corner of life when we're consistently happy, loving, joyful, optimistic, and passionate. These emotions quickly draw material abundance to us. They massage the heart and can create many miracles in a day, miracles of the *ooooh* and *ahhhhh* variety. Conversely, when we're angry, fearful, pessimistic, worried, sad, self-loathing, or depressed, we create our own personal purgatory.

Of all the emotions, anger and fear are the most destructive and the biggest trouble makers. If we knew the damage such hefty emotions had on our lives, we would be arrested for the premeditated murder of our own divine potential. The longer we simmer in anger and dwell in fear, the more financial breakdowns are likely to occur, the result of the prolonged negative thoughts and emotions. We're weary from the weight of such heavy emotions, moods so heavy they can dampen an entire football arena. We put a lid on abundance when we simmer in any sort of negativity. Ergo, the happier we are on a daily basis, the more abundance flows our way. Ain't it grand?

Here's a secret: our embrace of love and joy is our deliverance from financial woes. There is nothing more important than feeling loving and joyful on a consistent basis. When we make this our mission, we cannot fail. It all seems so simple…and it is. When we are in good emotional space on a consistent basis, we actually create an opening for all of life's goodness to freely enter our experience.

I stumbled and, oh, how I fell. Back then, fear and concern were the source of my agitation. Like the Black Death that wiped out half of Europe, I was devoid of possibility and was stunned hopeless. Unconsciously, I generated moods that were somber and heavy, a stark contrast to who I'd been in my younger days when I had been a full expression of joy and believed there was nothing I couldn't do. Years later when my life didn't turn out the way I'd hoped, I became a Debbie Downer, full of complaint, criticism, and negativity. I had a negative river flowing through my mind, and it fed the negative tributaries of my dark and sullen mood. My job search was stalled. I still had no source of income, and my fear only continued to skyrocket. My festering negativity became an opportunity blocker, and nothing was coming or going my way. Thankfully, I was delivered from the hell of my own mind once I took on the practice of joy on a daily basis. I began reveling in small wonders like watching my children sleep peacefully, gazing at the full moon, or listening to the choir of birds that chirped at day break. I basked in the sunrise, so full of yellows, oranges, and pinks, streaming in through my bedroom window setting the stage for my morning mind work. An invisible unfolding of peace occurred once joy began to emerge. My daily walks in the countryside made visible the bold and vivid majestic colors in the sky and the fields. I was the same, yet something was different. My drabby life was going from black and white to Technicolor; I felt like Dorothy emerging from her storm-tossed farmhouse in the land of Oz. Everything looked and felt so alive and vibrant. All the sights, smells and sounds were vivid. My joy was becoming exquisitely profound, and I felt my heart growing bigger. And suddenly the job opportunities began to appear, and so did some money. Halleluiah.

The exit route to contentment requires mastering your thoughts and emotions in such a way that they produce the results you want but it'll take you longer to get there unless you start managing those moods of yours. This may not be easy at first. Managing your thoughts and emotions may seem a bit like herding cats moving in different directions, especially if you're rifling with overdue bills. When you're in the midst of yet another financial crisis, barbed knots of fear, anger, anxiety, frustration, and disappointment may arise. You've conditioned your mind to respond to financial discord in this manner, and this is the negative programming in your brain that you're out to transform. Your current experience is based on previous thoughts and emotions. Thoughts and emotions create experiences, which create reactive thoughts and emotions, which lead to another experience, and on and on it goes. Once you change the inner experience of the outer event, the dismantling of the negative brain pattern can finally take place, and a new brain pattern emerges.

Love and joy will always lift you high above the limitations of the world. Any diversion from these two emotions is a diversion from abundance. Your mission is to deliberately choose the emotions that create magic instead of those that rip you apart from the inside out. Each time you intentionally choose a state of joy over despair you experience nothing less than the making of miracles. Your emotions are something you choose moment by moment. Master your emotions, and the details of your life will improve.

Lay down some new programming in that thick skull of yours. You have a date with destiny. You are now fasting from negative emotions. Stay away from those blasted bastards! And if you start to cave, get a friend to yell at you, so you can see how ridiculous it looks to wear such vile emotions. It may be tough, but you can do it! Good luck!

I manage my emotions. My emotions no longer manage me.

I can have anything I want in life. I simply need to place my attention on what I desire with frequency.

> "It's the repetition of affirmations that leads to belief. And once that belief becomes a deep conviction, things begin to happen."
> **- Claude M. Bristol**

> "The game of life is the game of boomerangs. Our thoughts, deeds and words return to us sooner or later, with astounding accuracy."
> **-Florence Shinn**

I now easily and effortlessly earn over $_____each year.

I can do anything.

TODAY'S GOALS

If you could remember how powerful you are in creating your reality, you would make different choices, have different conversations, think different thoughts, and feel different emotions. Be mindful of this throughout today.

_____
_____
_____
_____

THINGS FOR WHICH I'M GRATEFUL

I am enough. The greatest force there is created me.
I am perfect, whole, and complete just as I am.

_____
_____
_____

AFFIRMATIONS

Each day, my income is increasing in expected and unexpected ways.

Day 12 - Speaking it into existence

"We are what our thoughts have made us; so take care about what you think. Words are secondary. Thoughts live; they travel far." -Swami Vivekananda

Most people engage in conversational topics of lack on a daily basis. Misery sure does love some good company, doesn't it? Our words have creative power, and we misuse them by continuing to tell stories of lack, struggle, and our shortage of money. This only makes a ruckus trapping us in a financial no-man's land, and the negativity conquers like an army. And we want to call ourselves victims of circumstance? Really? We should have your mouths washed out with soap. Unless we cultivate the human mind with intentionality that pulls us far forward, the mind will simply react and respond to circumstances as it always has. Shall I give you an example?

Edith was persistent in her pursuit of abundance. She sought me out on the Internet, and after reading her email I was immediately taken with her boldness. We all cling to something, and hope and faith were the life preservers that buoyed Edith throughout the flooding of a lifetime of darkness. She was wrung out and fed up with never having enough money and said she'd do whatever was required to radically alter her financial circumstances. The woman was such a demand for coaching, I was certain it wouldn't take her long to meet some newfound success with money. She had fierce ambition despite the severe setbacks she'd encountered in life.

Years ago, Edith had become the first black woman to become a licensed master electrician, but her career went terribly awry when drug addiction confiscated everything she held dear. Her strong faith is what led her down the path to sobriety. Now a minister, Edith was looking for a church where she could plant some roots and make a difference for others. Shortly after she began the reprogramming of her mind, Edith had an interview at a church that she felt was perfect for her. She was absolutely certain the church would offer her a job. I was not at all surprised to hear how quickly things were unfolding for her.

When she called me a week later, her voice was flat and full of fear, a stark contrast from the enthusiastic woman I'd known her to be. A breakthrough in her finances didn't seem possible, she said. Edith wanted me to convince her that the exercises in the book would indeed work. I told her I wasn't about to convince anyone of anything. Whatever it is we choose to believe is precisely what occurs for us. Her emotions were dark. Of course, her thoughts were at the source. When I asked her what sparked her emotional spin downward, she told me she hadn't heard back from the church where she'd interviewed, and she was more disappointed than she'd ever been before. She went on to say that she didn't have enough money to pay her bills. She was broke. She was scared. Her negative rant continued, only now Edith wanted to tell me about a recent conversation she'd had with someone about the high number of electricians who are unemployed in the country, and just how unfair she thought it was.

I stopped the poor woman from her self-defeating rampage and asked her to notice what she had just said. She paused and said, "What? What did I say?" I repeated the last few sentences she spoke regarding her fear over not being able to pay her bills, about being broke, and about the irrelevant number of unemployed electricians. "Do you realize what you're doing? Do you realize you're powerfully and single-handedly creating your future with what you just said to me?" Finally, she went silent.

Edith is like a lot of us. Our complaints send us spinning, and until we get to the point where we've had enough of the emotional roller coaster ride, we will remain slaves to our own suffering. The negative dribble that flows so freely from our mouths perpetuates our own agony. It must end. To the extent of our own bullshit, we toss on a merciless storm of emotions. Serious humanness is at the helm. We come to a roadblock and claim foul, succumbing to our negative conditioning that fights back with a vengeance. It's too hard, we tell ourselves. It is here that we give up and quit, and it's absurd considering the wisdom and power we have within. If instead we seek to find our grail by pressing on in the face of adversity, personal transformation will emerge, and we will finally be redeemed. We must be bold and hold steady to the practices that change the way in which we think, feel, and speak; otherwise a lasting shift cannot occur.

We tell ourselves disturbing truths, and then we begin to believe them. Sometimes we can be just plain asinine. We love to complain. We are avid. All of the thoughts we think and the strong emotions we feel fuel our magic wands. It is in our speaking that we wave a wand to effect its magic into our lives, and we're going to face the consequences of that. Always. We speak our conversations right into existence. No wonder we're flat-lining from exhaustion much of the time. The terror really begins to ignite in our hearts once we share our internal negative chatter in our conversations with others. In doing so, we fall victim to external viewpoints. Who needs that?

Much of the time, we talk simply for the sake of talking. If you're one of these chatter boxes, *shut up*! Please, just shut up. There's no intentionality with your constant chatter. Unless you stop running at the mouth, you'll interfere with the work you're doing here.

Back to Edith and her wordy dilemma. I told Edith that it was no mystery why she was in a breakdown with her prosperity work as it was clear that her mental pollution was the result of thoughts running wild without any focused direction and her rapid fire negative conversation. When I asked how often she was doing the mental training, she said she had too many other things going on, and not having received an immediate job offer after the interview, she gave up on the mind work completely.

I explained to a calmer Edith that when we become so attached to what the perfect job must look like for us, we can end up shooting ourselves in the foot. The universe knows *exactly* what will serve our highest good, yet we become so fixated on what *we* think is best for us that we actually detract any goodness from making an appearance. Instead we can intentionally and consistently concentrate our mind power on abundance, and the universe will never fail to guide us to the perfect opportunities in direct alignment with the prosperity we're affirming for ourselves. All we have to do is be open and *allow* the prosperity in. If the church did not offer Edith the job she was strongly attached to, there was an even better job waiting for her, one far more magnificent than the one she had her heart set on.

We're either creating or complaining. In the fertile world of storytelling, we create in life whatever it is we passionately speak about. We construct boundaries and limitations by the stories we've created about ourselves. *I'm terrible with money. I work double time to everyone's single time, and I'm still no further ahead. I was never meant to be rich. I am always broke. I am so moody. I struggle paying my bills. Money seems to slip through my fingers. Nothing ever works out for me. Everything is so expensive.* Stop complaining. Statements such as these are like a dark spell, and they have creative power. What we have on our mind does not need to be shared with the world. The moment you recognize the negative story coming from your mouth, ask for a do-over and rewrite the dang story in a way you want your life to occur. Close your eyes and allow the God in you to say it for you. Any word that holds you back from abundance is now a forbidden word in your vocabulary, and you will no longer trespass on prosperity by abusing them.

Every breath counts and each moment matters. It is absolutely imperative to devote time to silence the mental pollution. Once you understand how this process really works, you can no longer play dumb. You're in control of your thoughts, your emotions, and your conversations. You're calling the shots. No one else does. Subject your mind to deep and detailed scrutiny and powerfully choose your thoughts. Think before you speak and deliberately choose the words with which you speak. By doing so, you tap into the direct pipeline to your success.

You no longer know the meaning of the words "being negative". Actually, you'll need to be excused from the dinner table for being so gosh darn positive. Heaven made you special, and you're wasting time not appreciating it. You just never know what's going to happen next. An avalanche of abundance is beginning to tumble your way, so make room for it. *Helloooooo, Destiny!*

I am destined for my very own brand of greatness.

I think my thoughts. My thoughts do not think me. I am the architect of my inner dialogue.

> "Every complaint is a little story the mind makes up that you completely believe in."
> **— Eckhart Tolle**

> "Practice rather than preach. Make of your life an affirmation, defined by your ideals, not the negation of others. Dare to the level of your capability then go beyond to a higher level."
> **- Alexander Haig**

I now easily and effortlessly earn over $_____each year.

You're either creating or complaining. Which are you doing?

TODAY'S GOALS
What are you choosing to accomplish today? There is nothing you can't do.

THINGS FOR WHICH I'M GRATEFUL
"Stop your agitated thoughts and find out who it is that stops them."
-Sri Ramana Maharshi

AFFIRMATIONS
Choose to shine.

Day 13- Your Words Create Your World

"Handle them carefully, for words have more power than atom bombs." -Pearl Strachan

May I be blunt? We've become a pack of jibber jabbers, freely sharing our noxious woes with anyone who will stop and listen, and once we have an attentive audience, the spewing of our every complaint, ailment, and frustration ensues. When we choose to create such fear and panic within our conversations, we induce others to join us in drinking the poison. The wise ones run like bats out of hell to steer clear of our toxic web. We certainly are liberal with our proclamations of the scorn and contempt we hold in our hearts when things don't go our way. Our petty preoccupations leave us stunted. Vulnerable to the darkness of such pessimistic programming, we've become negative ninnies, and it impinges on our ability to soar. Consider our conversations. Our words create or they destroy. We not only attack others but we attack ourselves, too. We condemn and we judge. We criticize. We complain often enough that we actually manufacture the complaints into our own experience. And if everything's going along too smoothly, we'll invent some pointless drama just to stir things up. God help us. This pollution of the mind fuels an invisible war with plenty of casualties, and it runs our goodness into the ground every time. No wonder we're borderline hysterical. What a waste it is keeping our view focused on the ground of our misery. In doing so, we keep hidden the capacities of our human potential. Put a sock in it, will you?

Our light will become brighter when we consciously guard all that we speak. Today, we're going to expand our personal power with a little word-to-word resuscitation. Whatever we put out there, we get back. Our words are a force. Our ability to speak is one of the powers we have to create; our words create our world. With them, we express our thoughts, opinions, and beliefs. We are so enormously powerful that we literally speak our words into existence; we speak it, and it becomes so. Our every intent manifests through our words, and our current financial circumstance is merely the direct manifestation of our inner thoughts, emotions and conversations. We're responsible for it all.

Since thoughts create our emotions, our spoken words transmit our emotional energy out into the world for physical creation. We draw to us the very things we think and speak about. If a foul mood settles in, our thoughts are at the source, and they cannot be positive. These poisonous thoughts create the negative emotions that are at the source of our lousy mood, and we take it one step further in the creation process when we verbalize our inner junk.

Those who speak of prosperity have prosperity in their lives. Those who speak of lack, experience lack in their lives. There's no denying this powerful law of mind, so stop denying it. We damn ourselves when we say things like, *"I can't afford to do that."* The venom in our words extends outward to the creation stage-a negative creation stage.

How many times do we awaken to a dull, gray, rainy day only to tell ourselves that the rest of the day is going to be just awful and downright depressing? How does that day then turn out? Is it a day full of enthusiasm and wonderful opportunities? I'm guessing it's not. We complain about the rainy day to everyone else too, thus spreading our negative venom to others as well. We only destroy ourselves by saying, *"I hate my job,"* as such a poisonous declaration determines exactly how you experience your job. It's your words about it, the way you describe it that determines how your job occurs for you. Declaring instead, *"I now have a job that I absolutely love, and I'm paid very, very well,"* will either attract to us a new job that is in alignment with the positive declaration or a profound shift will occur in the current work environment that's in alliance with the positive declaration.

We will continue to crash tragically by complaining about our financial condition. I know people who frequently share their negative money stories, and they do so with great passion and emotional conviction. This is self-sabotage as the negative money stories we tell, especially those fueled with strong emotions, will always manifest the negative scenario into our experience. This is how powerful our spoken words are.

I was having dinner recently with some friends, and the conversation turned towards the economy. My friend, Ross, announced that he was absolutely certain that another grave Stock Market crash was eminent, and it would be far worse than the one that began in 1929. He then went on to describe how he was preparing for it. I would not participate in that discussion. I took my head elsewhere. Having experienced all the great successes I'd met as a result of doing this work, I am fully aware of the creative power of words. We can certainly discuss the facts about what has already occurred in history, but I don't participate in conversations that cause me to be fearful about our economy. The economy is merely a reflection of mass consciousness, the common belief system held by so many others that it eventually manifested into societal reality. It does not matter what happens 'out there'. Whatever occurs out there will have no impact on my financial circumstances because I say it won't. It makes no difference if you're remembering the past, thinking about the future, or looking at what's taking place in your life right now, whatever you're paying attention to will cause the creation of it.

You cannot speak of lack and experience prosperity. If you speak of lack, you will experience lack. If you speak of prosperity, you will experience prosperity. If you say, *"I'm broke,"* then you have a belief that you are always broke. These words reveal a bankrupt brain pattern. When you believe you're always broke you think, feel, speak, and act out of this belief and set into motion tremendous creative energy. Verbalizing negative thoughts about money only feeds them more energy, more manifestation power. We're lured away from our real worth, our real power when we participate in negative conversations with others about our money deficits, the jobless rate, and the declining economy.

Our conversations are the birth canal of our thoughts and emotions, so let's put an end to the toxic commentary about how expensive things are, shall we? When we pay close attention to the words we use and the thoughts we think, we can easily see the brain pattern in place that's running our lives into the ground and must be taken out of commission. You'll fare much better by monitoring your conversations. Once we are consciously aware of the commanding impact of negative words and its leaden baggage, we won't fall victim to its darkness ever again.

You are the author of your own stories, so stop the negative dissertation of how bad your life is. It only takes one moment to change the tide. You'll save your own soul by gracefully backing out of the conversations that are negative and creating new conversations that spur you to greater achievement. Choose wisely the words with which you speak, and become a beautiful beacon of light by bringing some grace to your every conversation. You'll foster your own greatness and somebody else's by doing so.

Be mindful of the way in which you pronounce your state of being. The next time someone asks how you're doing, choose a great response back that you can live into like, *"I woke up on the right side of the bed!"*, or *"I feel good!"* or *"I love my life!"* Or *"I am incredible!"* You'll make magic appear right before your eyes, I swear. You'll feel fabulous. They'll feel fabulous. Yadda, yadda, yadda. On and on it goes.

We're God's little darlings, darlin'. Don't you get it? Stop looking for the magic. You *are* the magic, Boo! It is only when we become reacquainted and reconnected again to who we really are- love and pure joy-that we are fully empowered again to be the wildly creative masters we were born to be. Bring to a halt your pettiness and get up to something big. You are only visiting here, and it's high time you retrieve your personal power and begin reaching for all that is now possible. You're bungee jumping off the scale of abundance enhancing your human capacities. Trust me. You won't ever look back. Yeah, baby.

My words create my world.

I choose all of my conversations carefully.

I no longer engage in conversations about lack.

> "Reality is a projection of your thoughts or the things you habitually think about."
> **-Stephen Richards**

> "Watch your manner of speech if you wish to develop a peaceful state of mind. Start each day by affirming peaceful, contented and happy attitudes and your days will tend to be pleasant and successful."
> **- Norman Vincent Peale**

I now easily and effortlessly earn over $_____**each year.**

I feel good!

TODAY'S GOALS

Stop being stopped. You think you'll start playing big next week, but all you have is right now. Keep your eye on the prize and lean into the finish line, darlin'. The time is right now. Your quantum leap forward today creates a multitude of blessings that fall effortlessly into your little lap. Can you dig it? Uh-huh. I thought so. Now get moving. Consistent effort is the only way.

_____   _____
_____   _____
_____   _____
_____   _____
_____   _____

THINGS FOR WHICH I'M GRATEFUL

Be grateful for each small miracle. The way-bigger rock-star ones are coming.

_____   _____
_____   _____
_____   _____

AFFIRMATIONS

I allow myself to think and dream in unlimited ways. Anything is possible for me.

_____
_____
_____
_____
_____
_____
_____
_____

Day 14- The Art of Imagination

"Imagination is the beginning of creation. You imagine what you desire, you will what you imagine and at last you create what you will." -George Bernard Shaw

Frankly, my dear, you do give a damn. You're realizing this now. You have the Midas touch. You live by your own lights. You spin straw into platinum gold, and money, fame, dreams, and destiny are yours, if you want them. Comprender? Take a moment here, you bouquet of good fortune, and consider this proposition. What if I told you that spending a mere 5 minutes each day intentionally using your powerful imagination would grant you every single wish you wished after just 30 days. Would you do it? Of course you would. So do it.

Imagination is one of our greatest creative abilities. Reality is swayed when the power of the mind and the emotions are intentionally used in the imagination. By tapping into the inner realms, we tap into our inner gifts and cosmic capabilities. Nearly everything that we've done in life, we've first thought about doing it. To imagine something is to bring the image into being. It is in the imagination where we rehearse how it will feel once we achieve our goals, so if we frequently concentrate the imagination on the end results and feel joyful while we're doing it, the results appear swiftly.

Our imagination can be used to create good things for us or not-so-good things for us. Either way, whatever we spend time imagining will return to us. We've all been graced with the gift of imagination, but how we use it determines if we live an abundant life or one brimming with struggle. What you may have been doing up until this point is projecting in your imagination what the outcome of a stressful financial situation will be, imagining the way it will turn out, and all the things that may go wrong, and how we imagine everything we think we'll experience; failure, rejection, fear, poverty. Ugh. We create enough negative energy from thinking the awful thoughts, feeling the lousy emotions, and imagining the negative outcome that the ghastly energy now goes out to create our vision in life. We're left dead in our tracks…again. What's amusing about this is that then we justify the bad thing that we just created by saying, *"See! I was right! I now have proof!"* In a way, we are correct. The very situation we worried enough about actually manifested. This is how most of us play a significant role in creating our very own negative reality show. We do it through negative visualization, and the result is a mental mis-creation. Do you see how very powerful you are?

Think about the stories you emotionally immerse yourself in throughout the day. Are you perseverating on bills? Are you immersed in an intensive-care-level stress scenario of what it will be like if you don't come up with the money to get your car fixed? You cheeky contrarian-this is *negative* visualization. Indulging in this sloppy mind play takes you to the dark places and is a highly counterproductive use of your valuable time. We disturb inspiration with such images. Unconsciously imagining scenarios so full of negative emotion exterminates your success. Instead, heavily engage in an imaged scenario with a *positive* outcome and watch it manifest quickly into your existence. The more intense positive emotion you feel as you vividly paint the picture, the faster it occurs for you. Imagine and let go, knowing with full certainty that is now on its way.

You've been a veteran of a war that has no name. You've suffered enough. Ply the power of your mighty imagination to create all the good things you want to occur. Living debt free, increasing your income, or getting a new car or house can all be achieved by intentionally using your imagination. It's all in the details, dearie. The key here is to design something that quickly engages the imagination and fully concentrate on the details of it. Feeling strong, positive emotions during the visualization has a major impact in molding your reality.

You are never given a desire without having the power to make it true, you can be, do, or have whatever you can imagine. If you'd like to own a fancy schmancy new sports car, you begin the creation of it first by imagining exactly how the car looks, feels, and drives. What color is the exterior? What color is the interior? Be very specific. Is the car green with a camel interior? Or is it black with a grey interior? Are the seats cloth or leather? What does the dashboard look like? What does your new sports car smell like when you get into it? Does it have that new car smell or is it fragrant with rich, beautiful leather? Now imagine getting into the car, grasping the steering wheel, and driving it to wherever you want to go. Immerse yourself in the feelings of actually driving the car along a beautiful countryside. Are you excited? Thrilled? Can you feel your adrenalin levels rise? Now imagine yourself pulling into your driveway with your sports car. Allow yourself to fully feel and see the entire experience. That's all there is to it.

What are your dreams that are begging to be realized? The ones that have been locked away in your heart for so long that rigor mortis has set in. Manifesting is your birthright. Absolutely anything you want is just a little bit of thinking away. It's never too late to create anything you desire. That's the beauty of it. You can begin right now, this very second, and dream without boundaries, you wistful soul.

Whatever is possible in the mind is possible in reality. When you're imagining something, the brain doesn't know if what you're seeing is real or remembered from the past. Wherever you place your undivided attention on is what you will manifest. You're creating constantly, but most of the time you're not intentional with what you're creating, which is why you don't have a constant flow of money in your life yet. You haven't intentionally focused enough of your creative energy frequently enough on prosperity. The more you visualize what it looks like and feels like to have a constant flow of money, the more you condition your brain into believing you have a constant flow of money in your life right now in this very moment. It reinforces the new brain pattern you're in the process of creating with your money affirmations.

Action: Focusing Your Imagination

In a quiet space, in whatever posture is most comfortable for you, close your eyes, and take a few slow deep breaths. Relax and allow yourself to float along like a particle in a solution. Place all of your attention on the income amount you're requesting. See it clearly on the white screen of your mind. Repeat this dollar amount to yourself several times, "*$100,000, $100,000, $100,000*", or whatever the amount is you're focusing on. See it appear in your mind, and think only of this income amount. Silently repeat the income amount over and over again as you see it clearly in your mind and do this for approximately 30 seconds. Repeat this a few times throughout the day. You're practicing with the magic wand of imagination. With this, your ability to concentrate on the prosperity improves. Imagine often what you want your life to be, and it shall be.

Your imagination will always lead you through the dark. As a fabulous imagineer, you can create any income for yourself. Yes, *any* income. Because you've already received the income in your mind. *In your mind.* You see it done already, and it is. Whatever you imagine in your mind is waiting for you. Anything repeatedly held in the imagination is fully created in the invisible. For it to become visible, harness the great force of love by imagining and feeling what you love. It's that simple. What is it that you want to experience? An enormous balance in your checking account? A new car? A new career? A constant flow of money in your life? Whatever it is you want to create, prop yourself up in bed like you're the Queen of Sheba and get to work in that wildly rich imagination of yours, my lovepuff. And pepper it with love. Lots and lots of love.

Use the power of your rich imagination for a mere five minutes each day and see your life the way you want it to be because it is literally life-changing and reality altering. See images of money coming to you from absolutely everywhere. Visualize a large bank account balance. Imagine money filling the room. Bless the images in mental creation surrounding them with lots of love and light and release your vision to God. He'll take care of the rest. If you start spacing out, gently call your mind back.

Imagine and let go. See your dreams already coming true. Predicate your life from that stance and filter all thoughts and emotions from there. You'll unlock the codes that you carry that expand the awareness of who you are, why you are so important, where you've come from, what your gifts are, and the legacy you will leave. Out of thin air, the realization of your every desire will begin to take form. This is easy wisdom, so begin big with it today and in time, you'll be living it.

Imagine it. Pretend it. Dream on and dream big. Carpe the heck out of this Diem! You are a rainmaker. There's nothing you can't create. You're going places, kiddo!

The things I create are far better than I ever imagined.

All financial doors are wide open; an endless bounty now comes to me.

> "See things as you would have them be instead of as they are."
> **- Robert Collier**

> "Your imagination is your preview of life's coming attractions."
> **-Albert Einstein**

> "All the breaks you need in life wait within your imagination. Imagination is the workshop of your mind, capable of turning mind energy into accomplishment and wealth."
> **-Napoleon Hill**

I now easily and effortlessly earn over $_____each year.

TODAY'S GOALS

Write your affirmations. Go for a walk in nature and repeat them over and over. Use your imagination to envision the life you want to have. Manage your emotions. Only consistent effort will reap the financial rewards you're aiming for.

THINGS FOR WHICH I'M GRATEFUL

"The future you see is the future you get."
-Robert G. Allen

AFFIRMATIONS

The things I imagine frequently for myself always come true.
I charge my visions with love and excitement.

Day 15- Like Attracts Like. Like it or Not.

"The Law of Attraction will certainly and unerringly bring to you the conditions, environment, and experiences in life, corresponding with your habitual, characteristic, predominant mental attitude." - Charles F. Haanel

     Our function on earth is to create. It's why we have the magic that comes through us. Once we glimpse our spiritual magnificence, there is no going back. If we allow Spirit to take part in the creation process, our ability to create soars, yielding the most glorious manifestations. We are in a holy partnership with God. There is powerful energy within us all. God is always ready to respond when we intentionally use our gifts, and The Law of Attraction is the universal delivery vehicle of all responses. This is the natural order of the universe. It is cosmic law.

     Everything that exists in reality was a thought to begin with, and then form followed. The magic wands with which we were born create our physical outcomes. Every thought has energy, and spoken words, emotions, and imagination have even greater energy that alters our reality. The Law of Attraction is surprisingly simple: like attracts like. This immutable law of the universe is constantly at work whether or not we're aware of it. There is no such thing as a thought that goes unnoticed by the universe. Every thought, emotion, and image we focus on is met in kind.

     We can't see energy, hold energy, or sense energy through our physical senses in any definitive manner. We can certainly run low on energy, but we never run out of energy. Every human brain is a transmitter of energy, and absolutely everything is governed by our energy. What we focus on, what we emote about, is unerringly what we draw to us. Each of us is like a magnet, pulling into our world whatever we dwell upon in the mind. Energy is the raw material of creation, and it's everywhere waiting to be activated by our magic wands of thought, conversation, imagination, and the most potent wand of all-emotion.

     We are at the source of our own dilemmas. Nothing accidentally appears in our lives. We attract it all. There are no exceptions to this. Absolutely everyone and everything enters our experience by way of our thoughts, emotions, conversations and imaginings. Every person in your life is there because you have drawn them there. You get to choose what you do with them.

     The universe is always eavesdropping on your internal dialogue and will return to you the physical representation of those thoughts and feelings, and it can only reflect back exactly what it receives. The energy we extend outward draws to us the exact match in physical form. It is the energy of our emotions, our attitude, and our state-of-mind that determines if what we're attracting is positive or negative. The Law of Attraction boomerangs back to us whatever it is we feel the most strongly about. This is crucial knowledge. Since the mind is always our obedient servant, *what* we attract is dependent on the *type* of energy we emit. If we transmit negative energy, we attract negative circumstances. If we transmit positive energy, we attract positive circumstances. Simple enough.

     Everything we experience is subject to the energy we're transmitting, and nothing can enter our experience without our very own concentrated attention pulling it towards us. We reap what we sow, darling. Focused thoughts are the seeds we plant in the fertile soil of the mind. Our emotions, conversations and imaginings provide the watering for the gestation of the plant roots to sprout deep into the earth sending energy into orbit, in our lives, and the world. The Law of

Attraction does the rest. We have a thought, "Why did they charge me so much to fix my car?" If we become angry after focusing on such a thought, the energy of anger is created. We put the bill aside and go about our day, but the energy of our anger does not disappear once we move on to something else. Instead, this energy extends out into the universe, commingling and uniting with the universal creative energy that has properties similar to it, and it creates an energy field of anger that's now attached to us. We continue to strengthen this negative field of energy when we get angry again and again, until eventually the energy field becomes dominant enough to pull to us the physical representation of our angry energy-more unexpected bills.

The implication is obvious: the life you have is a preponderance of the positive or negative energy you've emitted over a period of time. Consider the rocky road of frivolous financial disasters and bear witness to the unsettling side effects created first in thought. You are full-out creator of it all.

One simple shift of your energy can shape your destiny. Ascension is simply the raising of your energy. You receive the ascending vibrations of spiritual energies that emanate from the minutes of spiritual depth. By slowing down and tapping into your internal wisdom, you control the collisions that are merely an extension of your own mind. It is here that you ascend the negative energy that powers the roller coaster ride of your financial heartaches, and the negative energy can finally dissipate.

The Law of Attraction always yields to you the breadth of your energy attracting upon yourself the nature of your thoughts and emotions. It isn't enough to simply want something; you must be intentional with your mind power and your emotions to deliberately attract it. The very impact on your ability to thrive lies within your emotional energy. Once you learn how to use your energy properly, golden opportunities begin to easily flow your way.

Whatever you want is just a little thinking and feeling away. The Law of Attraction deems this so. That which is like unto itself is formed. You get that which you concentrate on whether you want it or not, so intentionality is the key here. You can have whatever you want in life by intentionally manipulating and co-creating with this energy. If you frequently, repeatedly, and passionately dwell upon or focus on a positive thought, desire or goal, you generate enough positive energy our musings need for creation. You know the drill: laser focus your mind power on what you want to create; empower it with powerful positive emotions; imagine the outcome; and repeat, repeat, repeat. Such a simple routine alters your fate.

Cultivate your extraordinary potential by controlling your focus and being deliberate with your emotional energy. Do whatever it takes to manage your emotions the next time your heart starts pounding and you're shaking with fury. Be still, go silent, and meditate, allowing the energy of your soul to respond to the situation. With courage and perseverance, you'll make the climb from financial insolvency to financial abundance. Bravo, lovey! Forge ahead using your personal power; it is an always-accessible always -renewable source.

Now is the time of crossing the threshold into the deeper strata as a co-creative agent. You have immense value. You have a divine purpose. You are love. You are kind to yourself. You are bright, happy, blazingly confident, and brimming with passion. You already possess all you've ever needed. You love and approve of yourself. You appreciate your big, beautiful life. Every wish you've ever wished and each desire you've held in your heart comes from the remembrance of your own inherit radiance from deep within your heart. For you are the cosmos, and the cosmos is you. God's love for you is as timeless as time, and his universe is at your command.

People love to give me money.

I now easily and effortlessly earn over $_____each year.

TODAY'S GOALS

Get your house in order. Clean your car until it sparkles. They're a reflection of your own mind. The more organized you are, the more focused you'll become. Repeat your affirmations as you engage in any task today.

THINGS FOR WHICH I'M GRATEFUL

Reality is the physical manifestation on the outside of what you believe on the inside. Your entire life is a reflection of your inner dialogue. Change the inner dialogue, and your life must change.

AFFIRMATIONS
Nothing limits me.

Day 16- Tapping into the Energy of Abundance.

"Everything is energy, and that's all there is to it. Match the frequency of the reality you want and you cannot help but get that reality. It can be no other way. This is not philosophy. This is physics." -Albert Einstein

There is enough abundance for everyone to share and have plenty left over, and the source of this abundance isn't outside of us. It lies deep within. It's been there all along. We came into this world not as human beings but as spirits inhabiting a human body. We are made up of energy, and so is everything else, money included. Prosperity isn't something we achieve. It is something we tune in to. Once we tap into the energy field of abundance, it will flow like water in arid soil. You get exactly what you think, speak and feel about, whether you like it or not, whether you want it or not. The Law of Attraction will never fail to bring to us the exact match of our energy.

Thought is pure energy, and thoughts charged with emotional energy have enormous impact. Whatever it is you feel strongly about, you will experience. Emotion is the power that attracts; it is energy in action. When you have enough energy in action, you create matter. This is creation in the works.

All of our life experiences occur as they do because of the energy we generate and transmit, either consciously or unconsciously, through our thoughts, emotions, conversations, and our imagination. Depending on our frame of mind or mood, this energy will be either positive or negative. It is with mastery that we are able to intentionally cause this energy to be one or the other. Emotions fuel our magic wands with creative energy, so once we practice managing our own emotional energy effectively, we can manifest anything we want and relatively quickly.

When we ruthlessly toss and rifle feeling agitated and shirty with our finances, we're summoning negative energy to support the unsettling side effects of financial disarray. Negative emotions have intense energy, and they move forward to create physical realties quickly-more financial conundrums. This equation always holds true: gorging on negative thoughts and feelings causes a swift decent to a nasty mood, and financial disruptions are the result of our own prolonged negative state of mind.

Fear and anger are especially powerful creative energies. When the subconscious mind continually receives negative impulses caused by fear and anger, it duplicates in life whatever it was instructed to manifest-the precise negative circumstances that cause more fear and anger. We thought the negative thoughts, we spoke the negative words, we felt the negative emotions, and we imagined the negative outcome, consequently giving our full attention to the very thing we did not want to occur for us. This is negative creation. We will no longer play so small. It is here we draw the battle lines.

Dormancy and resignation have visited us all at one time or another, but worrying rips us right out of our recliners and throws us into a hell we never saw coming. This pesky little culprit instigates the imagination to create what *we do not want to occur.* Yikes! Worrying derails our greatness. Anger and fear only create darkness in our lives.

Love and joy, on the other hand, are a horse of a different color. They always prevail over darkness. When we're emitting positive energy fueled by love, optimism, and joy, we emit a beautiful field of positive energy that draws to us the physical representation of that positive energy. It is in this force field where abundance exists, and this is the space we want to inhabit. You'll increase your energy levels by placing your attention on things of a higher nature, like beauty, joy, love, affinity, and creativity. When we experience compassion, love, and a divine connection to others, peace permeates the mind and floods the heart. Peace of mind puts us in the receiving state of abundance. It is with practice that we become proficient at invoking good-feeling emotions of joy, love, peace of mind, and happiness at will. If these emotions are practiced often enough, we become joyful, loving, and peaceful on command. This is emotional mastery.

You must change the process internally before it can be reflected externally in the world. You're no longer simply reacting to circumstances. Your return to emotional sobriety is inevitable. As soon as you accept the importance of managing your moods, your financial reality alters.

Don't fret if you're still experiencing the residual effects of your negative programming. This is temporary and will end sooner than later once you're intentional about emotionally reacting differently to your circumstances. Shift your energy, and your counterproductive mood shifts as well. If we're consistently feeling and thinking positively about something, it's impossible for it to turn out badly. Every time you intentionally choose a state of happiness over despair, heaven applauds your efforts as you raise your thoughts and soften your heart. This is where you'll find your internal power. Practice this enough, and you can pull money out of forever. The next time you go spinning from another financial hiccup, a quiet little ascension will do the trick. Take several slow, deep breaths and choose to emotionally respond to the situation differently. Write your affirmations when the worry warts hover. This will help. Make a request for divine assistance and allow pure and sacred silence to break the vicious cycle. When we quiet the mind, we are able to respond to God's guidance.

Manifestation is the ability to bring about whatever it is you feel strongly about. To manifest something, be very clear about what it is you want to create. Picture this in your mind and surround the image with love and continue nurturing it with love and more love

You're back on the radar. Now, it's your time to fly. You'll be offered something for free. You may win something. You'll find money in a parking lot, and it'll feel as good as Christmas. These are signs that reveal the impulses of Spirit made manifest. Applaud your progress. You're reclaiming joy, and very soon you'll ride like the wind.

I think and speak only of abundance.

My moods are important in the creative process. My moods are always positive.

How I feel is more important than anything else. I practice being consistently happy today.

> "We are just an advanced breed of monkeys on a minor planet of a very average star. But we can understand the Universe. That makes us something very special."
> **- Stephen Hawking**

I now easily and effortlessly earn over $_____each year.

I live a life I love.

TODAY'S GOALS

Set a timer for 30-60 minutes today and complete all the tasks you don't want to do. Knowing you have a limited amount of time to complete them will spur you into mega action. And voila! You'll complete them easily

_____

_____

_____

_____

THINGS FOR WHICH I'M GRATEFUL

Everything exists for joy. Feel gratitude and joy for all the goodness in your life right now.

_____

_____

_____

AFFIRMATIONS

I concentrate fully on thoughts and images of abundance throughout the day.
Money is drawn to me.

What you fully concentrate on comes back to you as a perfect match.

Day 17 - Our Personal Energy Crisis

"Each of us sends out positive or negative vibrations, often without being conscious that we are doing so. What if we made an effort to be consciously positive, to resonate messages of the highest good for others and ourselves? What if we made a deliberate attempt to keep our thoughts aligned with God's spiritual optimism, to refuse to be stuck in self-centered fear? Our thoughts speak louder than our words. In order to change what we create, we must change our thinking. We must mind our mind." - Albert Clayton Gaulden

How's your mood today? I mean, really? Have you made any progress managing your emotions yet? In hectic modern living, our days speed along so quickly it's like being hurled into the abyss, and the rhythm never ends. It only seems to strengthen and expand, leaving us frantic most of the time, and the darkness that we know feels like a curse. We hang on in quiet desperation waiting to be lifted from the shadowy spell. Our power has been so misused and mishandled that we're zapped of any creative energy. Ours is a personal energy crisis enslaving us in a continued struggle with money. What's happening in our minds is happening outside of us, and until we purify our thought forms and rearrange our personal energy, we'll remain monetarily enslaved.

Our personal power is a gift from God. Our magic wands can create the most beautiful heaven or the most unforgiving hell. We barely survive our days expending enormous amounts of our personal energy through fear, anger and anxiety. We are each responsible for our own energy. No one else can influence this. Yet we tolerate these expensive feelings doing little to transform them. We use the power of our thoughts to generate seething emotions, and we use the power of our words to curse, destroy, complain, and blame. When such colossal power generated in the mind comes wickedly out of our mouths, we fuel our magic wands with such toxicity that we pull ourselves further into a hell of our very own creation. A spell is cast on our financial condition with such incorrect use of our power. It's of little surprise why we're so exhausted. When will we stop?

Everything is attraction based, and our attitude, our state of mind, and our emotions are how we attract absolutely everything to us, both good and bad. Our energy is contagious. The energy we emit pulls towards us the things, the people, and the circumstances that are a match to the energy we're transmitting. If you feel negatively toward anyone or anything, you're lowering your energetic resonance, and when you generate from this lower vibrational energy, you experience roadblocks, disappointments, illness, accidents, and a sense of being out of sync. Fear and anger are negative emotions that end up ruining our lives. They are relentless in their depletion of our personal power, and the high price we pay is more financial havoc. Ours is a personal energy crisis, and an intervention is crucial.

We're constantly transmitting energy through our thoughts, emotions, conversations, and imaginings that extend outward into the universe, where they mix and mingle with energy of its own kind and return to us more powerfully. Determining whether our energy is positive or negative isn't difficult. All there is to do is notice the emotions we're having: our feelings tell us everything we need to know about our connection to the unlimited creative power we can access.

Our personal power is restored to us as we sleep, and we awaken revitalized and ready to go with our daily supply of energy. And how do we spend that energy? Thoughtlessly, most of the time, as most of us unconsciously commence on a foolish spending spree of fear, anger, concern and worry. Is this you? You wake up feeling miserable about the job you must go to, and thoughts of dread begin to rant through your mind until the atmosphere in your head is not good. You argue with your spouse about an overdrawn checking account as you're getting dressed. Your pants feel tighter from your recent weight gain, so you begin to hate and reject yourself for being so fat. Now you're on your way to work, and you curse the other drivers as they cut you off on the highway. You feel the fire in your belly as you flip them the bird. The majority of your day is spent in misery. You go into a deeper hell after you arrive home and open the mail... and on and on it goes. When your personal energy is tainted with such toxic negativity, you extend it outward through your magic wands. No wonder you're broke. *You're giving away your power, dear human.* You are the cause of your reality, and everything that occurs for you correlates with the essence of your energy. You are responsible for whether your energy is of a higher vibration or a lower vibration.

Love, joy and gratitude significantly alter your energy field. They are the strongest forces that exist, and it is with them that we claim our personal power to create abundance everywhere. Love, joy and thankfulness grant a life so full and magnificent-a life so incredibly rewarding. They are the tools of real magic. The drama of our own personal hell will finally come to an end and all of our power returns to us tenfold when we source love and joy. It is here where we are set free.

Play with your personal energy today. There's nothing you can't create quickly when you're generating love, joy, and gratitude on a consistent basis. Feel the energy pulsating through your body, and charge this energy with so much positivity that you alter everyone near you. There's so much beauty and love all around you. Focus your eyes there and don't ever leave. Resolve to live your life through love. The more you love, the more powerful you become. Allow love and unbridled joy to elevate and energize you above all negativity, and your magic wands will craft the loveliest life you can imagine for yourself.

Once you embrace the power and authority of your role as a divine soul, you are open to receiving all the blessings of abundance the universe has to offer. There's a new world waiting to be found, and you're realizing you're somehow part of it. You can feel the ground underneath you. Look up into the endless sky. The earth is holding you up. You feel lighter, and you can actually see the love coming from everything and everyone. Today, choose to be the source of love, joy, and gratitude in every situation. Go on. Give it a whirl. I wish you such brilliant success.

I am a miracle.

I am in full control of my thoughts, emotions and imaginings.

I always have more than enough money to pay my bills.

> "Fear, conformity, immorality: these are heavy burdens. They drain us of creative energy. And when we are drained of creative energy, we do not create."
> **-David McCallum**

I now easily and effortlessly earn over $_____each year.

TODAY'S GOALS

Think of one area of life that makes you feel the most uncomfortable, and that's where you'll find the biggest opportunity for expansion. Create some action items that put you out on the skinny branches. You can do this!

THINGS FOR WHICH I'M GRATEFUL
Imagine yourself as you would like to be.

> "People spend too much time finding other people to blame, too much energy finding excuses for not being what they are capable of being, and not enough energy putting themselves on the line, growing out of the past, and getting on with their lives."
> **-J. Michael Straczynski**

AFFIRMATIONS
I now attract the perfect job with the perfect income.

Day 18 - Man is a Machine

"Man is a machine, but a very peculiar machine. He is a machine, which, in right circumstances, and with right treatment, can know that he is a machine, and having fully realized this, he may find the ways to cease to be a machine. First of all, what man must know is that he is not one; he is many. He has not one permanent and unchangeable 'I' or Ego. He is always different. One moment he is one, another moment he is another, the third moment he is a third, and so on, almost without end." - P.D. Ouspensky

It's a bit unsettling, isn't it? Human beings function much like a machine. Essentially, the mortal mind is the machine, we aren't. We are vastly powerful spiritual beings created by God. Creative in nature, we were born to thrive. Our beautiful ethereal souls are housed in a skin sack called the human body, and the human body is operated by the human brain. We've believed the mind is us, but it isn't. We descended to this earthly realm to create and experience our lives in any way we choose, and within each of us lies the power of our consent to prosperity and to poverty. It is we who control this and not any other human being.

The human mind involuntarily reacts to stressful financial situations based on the brain patterns we have in place. The furnace breaks, the mortgage is overdue, or whatever it is that causes us to fraternize with monetary doom, and the machine- the brain begins to react. *Why do horrible things like this always happen to me? I don't have enough money to pay that bill! I never seem to get ahead. I'm the unluckiest person ever to be born. Life is just too hard.* Ladies and gentlemen, meet the dark passenger in your cranium: the voices. The dark passenger begins drowning us in a pool of negative emotions, and the senseless spending of our energy in anger, frustration, and worry ensues. The machine has taken control. We've been hijacked by the voices, and the voices always want to stop us. They want us to sit this one out and continue the struggle with money. The mind is like a prison. It generates the voices in our head that unleash the sadistic emotional reactions to the financial circumstances we're experiencing, and we're always left powerless to their vengeful attack. This is the condition of the human mind, and it is the source of all our suffering.

To a great extent, we are the products of our environment and the beliefs formed during our early years and from a lifetime of experiences. The human mind puzzles over everything, always seeking to create scenarios that fit into what the brain has experienced in the past. This makes sense to the brain. We're acting as if today were yesterday. All our assumptions and thoughts and emotions are retrieved from the stored memory banks in the brain, so all current thoughts, emotions and images from our imagination are all generated from past experiences.

The mortal mind tends to be serious and sad, so when we begin to lose hope and lose sight of our dreams, the despair grows stronger. Those with no hope are easy to control, so the machine takes over and any sign of soul life goes missing. Resignation, anger, depression, and bitterness are now in charge. It's a tree we can all hang from.

It is when we pay attention to the voices of fear, doubt, and worry that we fall under a dark spell. Under this spell, the parroting voices hint at our doom and fiscal Armageddon, and we're left too petrified, too disempowered, and too exhausted to respond powerfully to the financial hiccup. The voices tell us something is bad wrong, we're screwed, it's hopeless, and we believe it all. We fall so far into the dominant groove of fear the voices have created that we can't crawl out. This is something we've struggled with our entire lives.

All right, enough. It's retarded what we, as human beings, do to ourselves. When will you realize a brain pattern is firing your reactions? It's not you. It's the voices. They're not real. You simply hadn't known any better. Poor thing.

Why does it take a major accident or some catastrophic event before we open our eyes and begin living our lives on purpose instead of by default? Get with the program! If your finances aren't occurring in the way you want them to occur, the machine, your mortal mind, is running by default feeding the craziness. Your brain is always living in the past and responding to present situations with past data, and you behave as if you have no choice in the matter. You always have a choice, yet you continue to tolerate the symptoms. It's not what you do to your finances that's the problem; it's what you do to your mind. The ingrained money brain patterns you allow to run rampant perpetuate the financial lack. If you don't get intentional about taking charge of the machine, the machine will take charge of the situation. This is how the mortal mind works. Once the machine is in control, you're left powerless until you *choose* to take the wheel. The choice is always yours.

Duality and separation are conditions of the machine. Our identity keeps us separate from who we really are, and we cannot serve two masters. We've become blind to our own brilliance. Outside of divine alliance with who we really are-joyful, creative beings intended to thrive-we become vulnerable to the devices of the machine. God help us. We are divine souls; anything that says otherwise is the machine. Any negativity, fear or doubt we experience is the voice of the machine. Joy is our natural state, and it is in being joyful that we gain real momentum in the prosperity creation process. The moment that we allow love to pour from our hearts all misperceptions are cleared, and the calcification of the mortal mind is dissolved. The voices only serve to put the mind on loudspeaker, distracting us from creating prosperity. If you're tired, depressed, or fearful you're in bed with your mind. The voices can be that seductive.

Part of your ethereal mission is learning how to transcend the voices. Until you control the mind, the endless cycle of financial lack perpetuates. You won't add to the drama by listening to the hawking voices. That's right. You *will not* pay attention to them. Instead you'll transcend their negative rant by acknowledging they are not real. They are the product of a defunct brain pattern. You'll tell them to get out. Beat it. *"Go ahead, fear and shame. Give me your best shot. I can take anything you can dish out, you nasty buggers!"* All there is to do is distinguish the voices of your negative emotions as they appear; acknowledge that they're on an invisible mission to stop you in life; pull your attention away from them and rise above them. No longer must you grit your teeth and bear the discomfort and suffering the voices never fail to bring. Instead allow them, and intentionally choose to think *over* them with thoughts of love and perpetual optimism. From now on, every time you move through them will be a victory.

Here's some good news to ponder, you fast rebounder, you. You're on the verge of a stunning comeback, and the amount of time it takes to get from where you are now with your finances to where you want to be is only the amount of time it takes you to choose who controls the machine. The operator of the machine calls all the shots and ultimately determines the outcome of each and every situation we encounter in life.

If you want to remove a problem from your life, simply relax and remove it from your thinking. That's all there is to it. You can create the life you want with thoughts founded in love and abundance. Develop your mind power by controlling your point of focus and big beautiful blessings will be delivered unto you. You can release the death grip of the voices and replace them with lovely affirmations that will carve out a brand new brain pattern that speaks prosperous voices, and they'll be music to your ears.

I control my thoughts: I think my thoughts. They do not think me.

The voices in my head are just voices. It's the way every human brain is wired. They are not real.

I always find money. I always get the best parking spaces.

People always offer me things for free.

> "The mind is like a machine that never shuts down. Does the engine on your car or your vacuum cleaner work incessantly, 24 hours a day? Why does your mind work this way?"
> **-Sri Ramana Maharshi**

> "Fear is the mind killer. Fear is the little death that brings total obliteration. I will face my fear. I will permit it to pass over me and through me. And when it has passed, I will turn the inner eye to see its path. Where the fear has gone there will be nothing. Only I will remain."
> **–Frank Herbert**

I now easily and effortlessly earn over $_____ each year.

Every day, in every way, my life just keeps getting better and better.

TODAY'S GOALS
What a pretty little package you are.

_____ _____
_____ _____
_____ _____

THINGS FOR WHICH I'M GRATEFUL
Thank you, God, for the abundant gifts you provide for me every day.

_____ _____
_____ _____
_____ _____

AFFIRMATIONS
I am always at the right place at the right time.

_____
_____
_____
_____
_____
_____
_____
_____
_____
_____

Day 19 - Having our emotions vs. being our emotions

"You are in charge. You have the ability to master your destiny." -Michael J. McCarthy

It's hell this morning, but it was pure heaven last night. Another bad mood has arrived, and it's taken us prisoner yet again. We go a little nutsoid when moods so foul overtake. We begin hyperventilating and splotching up from the stress we endure from it all. We're so angry we could spit. It's unspeakably offensive, the emotional tailspin that renders us powerless. *"Why do I even try? I'm too stupid, fat, unlucky, and lazy to make it. I don't have what it takes. I can't do it. There's no sense in even trying. I'll fail at whatever I try. I always do."*

Like a symphony that begins loudly, then slides into subtle entangling developments that grow on them, the voices of fear, anger, worry, doubt, and disappointment have thwarted more dreams that we will ever know. These small, self-doubting messengers return to pitch their all-too-familiar monologue. They're vacuous, vile, dumb, and dumber. They're quite a rowdy and devious pack. The mind plays hella tricks on us, doesn't it?

My God, pull yourself together. Don't you get it, doubter? The voices are just voices. They aren't real. They are the voices of the machine. They only seem real. They'll always be in your head. Everyone has them. It's what the human brain does.

The human brain operates in fight or flight mode in order to keep us alive, to protect us from danger. It was designed this way and has functioned in this manner throughout the evolution of the human being. But we no longer need to survive an attack by a saber tooth tiger or the jostle with a hungry bear. Nope. Bankruptcy and overdrawn checking accounts are the contemporary woolly mammoths we wrestle with these days. Yet, we're still heavily armed with strong, debilitating emotions that cause our fight or flight reactions to financial situations. When we allow the voices to run on autopilot, the mind dwells in emotional chaos and serves fear to protect the host: us. This is the function of the human brain. Fear puts such a stranglehold on us that the mortal mind is like an unruly child, throwing temper tantrum after temper tantrum. Bathed in thunderous emotions, the mind seeks to destroy our hopes and dreams. When does it end? *Dear human, everything that you are afraid of you've made up.*

You unknowingly adopted the dysfunctional money beliefs of others. Your thoughts and emotions of these money beliefs created the brain pattern that has brought you misery your entire life. Most importantly, what you're thinking pales in significance to what you are feeling. Your emotions are expressions of embedded pathways in the brain and play a pivotal part in this work. By managing your emotions you harness the creative power they hold. Continuing to emotionally react to your money dilemmas as you always have-with anger, fear, and worry-only reinforces your brain's patterns. No one can get you out of a situation: get yourself out.

How to dismantle it and create a new one that draws prosperity to you? Respond to your money issues as you never have before. When you choose to respond differently to a situation that previously would have sent you into a swirling basket case, a substantial shift takes place. In any situation, you have the power to choose how you respond. The mastery of your mind power comes from intentionally choosing how you respond emotionally to all financial upsets.

Strong emotions like love and joy/anger and fear, are extremely powerful creative forces. You decide what a situation is going to be for you. You can choose to respond with love, or you can choose to respond with the absence of love. Your emotional and financial freedom is dependent on which choice you make. There is no such thing as a problem without a blessing or two tagging along. Lift yourself high enough to see beyond the horizon, knowing that every situation bears a gift for your spiritual and financial growth.

I've suffered more than my fair share of drama in my life, and I was no victim. I recognize now that I was the source of all emotional malpractice. I won't give you any rah-rah bull hockey about being capable of managing your emotions at all times. There are times you become so consumed in doom and gloom that you can't pull yourself out of the rut, and the harder you try to stop the negative feelings, the fiercer they become. It won't matter how many affirmations you repeat. You're resisting the emotions by forcing them to be something other than what they are-negative emotions triggered by fearful thoughts. Our emotions happen to us; they are not us. The sooner you can distinguish this, a separation can occur between you and the emotion, and it will not overpower you any longer.

You may get triggered by nasty people or the trip to the hospital when you have no health insurance, and the negative emotions alive with a vengeance. Transcend them by invoking the forces of love and joy, and never again will you succumb to their negative tirade. The next time you're confronted by fear or anger, place your attention on your heart and feel the love that you were born with. Feel the love pulsing through your body and extend it out into the world. By doing so, you shift your personal energy. Continue to do this again and again and again until your mood is elevated above the roar. Each time you elevate our mood, you are in that very nanosecond aligning with the mothership.

For years, you've been feeding off the most rampant energy of darkness, squalor and pointless negativity. You no longer choose to indulge in such things. Your real power lies in deliberately choosing to *have* your emotions instead of *being y*our emotions. There's a big difference between the two.

When we're *being* our emotions, we're dominated by them. We shrink. We give up. We avoid. We withdraw. We wallow. We lash out at others in an effort to take them into hell with us. They become a driving, compulsive reaction to our circumstances. Forcing them away only feeds them more power. When we're *having* our emotions, we manage them responsibly by simply *allowing* them to be there. There's nothing to fix. There's nothing to change. There's nothing to do. This is the space of full empowerment. We can experience the emotions, but we're able to remain in action.

Consider sadness: nothing goes as deep as this emotion. Sadness gives you depth and provides insights about yourself that you didn't have before that only sadness can reveal. When you feel sad, simply notice that sadness is present. Allow it, embrace it, and sit with it. There isn't anything wrong with it. You can even give yourself permission to fully express the sadness by crying a river to release its powerful energy from your body. You don't need to make yourself wrong and beat yourself up for experiencing another negative emotion. You can simply notice the negative emotion you're having, acknowledge its presence, and allow it to move through you at its own pace. It will eventually dissipate. Until it does, the emotion won't dominate you as it has in the past.

> **Action:**
> Your breathing is a dependable indicator of your state of mind, and it's a good way to gauge your emotional status. As babies, our breathing was naturally deep and rhythmic. Observe the breathing of an infant and notice his stomach rising and falling with each breath. As stressed out adults under enemy fire, we breathe high in our chests taking shallow, choppy breaths that utilize but a small fraction of our lung capacity. Shallow, erratic breathing is the indicator of a fast moving, erratic mind. When things head south and start to unravel quickly, put some good clean oxygen into your lungs to restore your sanity. Begin by slowing down your breathing and focusing your mind on your breath as you take ten slow, deep breaths in the abdominal region. To center yourself in the midst of chaos, take three slow deep breaths. This works, I swear.

The mortal mind is an incredible machine of great complexity. It is a divine creation of God, and if honored as such a superb divine creation, you can use it to create wondrous things. There's only beauty, love, and joy to create, yet it's impossible to create anything great, especially abundance, when the mortal mind is still reacting to circumstances in fight or flight mode. Erupting in anger or running in shame when financial havoc attacks our peace of mind is a flawed decision. No longer do you invest in such emotions. You have within yourself the resources to create whatever kind of life you'd like. You are that powerful. You've just forgotten where you come from and who you really are. *It is not at all impossible to alter your fate.*

Listen up, kiddo: It's a bad idea to walk around in that head of yours. Stay out of there and turn your cheek to the noisy head clatter. When you feel like quitting, you're paying attention to the voices in your head. Herein your mastery is developed. Your moods are your direct access to abundance. If you're frightened by the current financial disaster that's assaulting, throw yourself on the mercy of the court and get out of your internal state of mind. Allow not fear to deter you. Instead, allow it to hone you. There is no challenge that is bigger than you. None. Ever. Your mental toughness is becoming exceptionally mind-blowing. You've been training for it and using it to your advantage these days, and emotions no longer dominate you. No matter how lost, scared, vulnerable, or powerless you have felt, you can choose every moment as a portal to peace, wisdom, and love. Between fear and unbridled power, there appear great winds of change, and they spell happy days ahead.

My emotions are mine to control. I choose to respond with love to all situations.

> "If your emotional abilities aren't in hand, if you don't have self-awareness, if you are not able to manage your distressing emotions, if you can't have empathy and have effective relationships, then no matter how smart you are, you are not going to get very far."
> **-Daniel Goleman**

I now easily and effortlessly earn over $_____ each year.

I love my life!

TODAY'S GOALS
"Man is a goal seeking animal. His life only has meaning if he is reaching out and striving for his goals."
-**Aristotle**

THINGS FOR WHICH I'M GRATEFUL
I walk, talk, look, act, think, and FEEL rich all day long! Woo Hoo!

AFFIRMATIONS
All of my affirmations manifest in the perfect way for the highest good of all concerned.

Day 20 - The Divine Plan

"We give up what we want to give up and keep what in some way we still want to keep. There are payoffs for holding on to small, weak patterns. We have an excuse not to shine. We don't have to take responsibility for the world when we're spending all our time in emotional pain. We're too busy. The truth that sets us free is an embrace of the divine within us." -Marianne Williamson

My God! I'm sorry you've endured such a distressing adulthood! Time after time, you've sat around and moped, feeling sorry for yourself after hitting all those unfortunate bumps in the road. Such negativity festered long enough that you unknowingly allowed the machine to take over, and, boy, did you stumble for days trying to regain control. It's bad crazy what we do to ourselves, isn't it? Bah! We just sit back in casual indifference twiddling our thumbs, waiting to see how things will pan out. No wonder our progress has been at a snail's pace.

Here's the deal: We're either passively sleeping through life or we're taking an active role in it. Those who take an active role in life find their experience much more interesting; they reap joy from their day-to-day living, and they easily create abundance. Passive or active. It's a choice. *You've had choices all along the way, humanoid.*

Life hurts sometimes. We feel so restricted, so cramped, and so frightened that we see no solution to our problems. But there is nothing to figure out. No puzzle to solve. No riddle to decipher. We've spent far too much time in our head and sinking further into chaos as a result of it.

Toxic energy is alive in our cities, in our neighborhoods. So many are living in fear, pain, sorrow, and anger. There's rage on our highways, more and more people living in poverty, and unhappiness so dire that addictions run rampant. Many are desperate to find joy, but they look for joy in all the wrong places.

Joy is within each of us. It's in our soul. Big time joy is waiting to be discovered and used in our mortal life. It is what unleashes luminosity into the world. We must tend to our own backyard before our efforts branch out further. We must cultivate our true essence, our true magnificence- only then can it blossom all around us.

Starting over, settling, and surviving. It was only when I had been brought to my knees by profound sorrow and rejection through my personal sagas that my wings expanded so much. I've gone down many different and varied paths during the course of my lifetime. Some were incredibly painful. Many were chock full of so much happiness it should have been illegal. The experiences that brought me the most pain and dropped me to my knees were the ones that ultimately caused the biggest personal transformation and provided me direct access to my own brand of happiness. I was always being led further down the path of my spiritual journey. I just didn't know it at the time.

You've searched and searched, but still can't seem to find your divine purpose in life. Your purpose has not been hiding from you. It only feels that way. Each part of your divine plan is revealed at precisely the right time according to your readiness. You are not stuck in the middle of nowhere, without clarity of who you really are. For ages, you've been playing the waiting game, and nothing appears to be changing. Though, you're quickly learning that nothing is as it seems.

Mysterious divinity lies in the unknown. You won't have to wait much longer to find your hidden treasure. Your treasure has been buried underneath an avalanche, and you've been on a search-and-rescue operation for several weeks. You've been so busy sending search parties out into the ethers and beyond. But the treasure you seek is hidden in the depths of your own back yard, and only you can find it. You can rely on your guardian angels to show you where to dig. To hear their direction, however, you must silence the mind chatter. The noisy distractions may call to you. Keep your eye to the sky and your ears close to the ground, you'll hear the direction. Listen well and ignore the voices. Their aim is to divert you far off course in any way they can. You choose to follow or not follow the misleading trail they always try to steer you down. Those dirty bastards.

For so long, you'd been self-forgetful, often wandering into the land of poor memory. Now you feel the pull of the strength hidden deep beneath the surface you've been treading upon completely unaware of until recently. You're close, so close you can feel it. You've switched your radio from 'transmit' mode to 'receive' mode. You can hear the signals honing you in on your target.

What you love is directly linked to your purpose. If you explore all the things that bring you joy you will surely find it. Whatever you feel most drawn to, you must go there; the path will unfold one step at a time. Love and joy will always elevate and energize you to pursue the highest value of your human spirit.

Life is far more interesting when you live it in love. When your heart bequeaths love, your body absorbs this love and then begins to know love. Your heart expands and the warm blossom of the divine light and love of God refuels you with strength once again. It is your fate to be light as air, to merge the soul with the heart, and to live each day in a continual state of unconditional love. The love you discover for yourself in this groundwork leads to the place where all things are accessible and all paths are easily seen. Remember to always follow your heart, braveheart.

It's no use relying on some external power to change you; you must change yourself. The training you've undergone during this correspondence course in prosperity has been rigorous, indeed. You've delivered some incredible results already. As you progress along the journey, mastering your magic wands through great self-discipline, the road before you is made manifest.

Shine like the shooting star you were born to be. Your life is getting bigger and better by the nano-second. My God, you're incredible. The time to soar is now.

I am always at the right place at the right time.

> "There is a plan for each of us, and each of us is precious. As we open our hearts more and more, we're moved in the directions in which we're supposed to go. Our gifts well up inside of us and extend of their own accord. We accomplish effortlessly."
> **- Marianne Williamson**

I now easily and effortlessly earn over $_____each year.

TODAY'S GOALS
I have surrendered to a greater capacity within me.

THINGS FOR WHICH I'M GRATEFUL
There is no shortage of money in my life. Ever.

When you emotionally react to a situation or a person, your brain is simply assessing the situation or person and retrieving data from your memory bank from a similar past experience. You will be tempted to react in the way you did before. This is the machine at work. You are a soul housed in the machine. Choose instead to respond to the situation or person with your soul.

AFFIRMATIONS
I can create anything I want. I am powerful beyond measure.

Day 21 - All You Need is Love.

"Life in abundance comes only through great love." -Elbert Hubbard

You are here for a reason. Baby, you were born to love. You *are* love. It's what you were created to be. It is the greatest of powers, a blessing from God that allows us to cross any hurdle in life and to bless the world. We are Divine. We are love and joy, and we will make our mark on this world when we follow our intuition and passions.

The problem is we think we are a great deal less than who we really are. We've been struck with amnesia. Love jogs our memory, reminding us from where we came. It is everything exquisite and divine. Our inherent nature is unconditional love, but we don't remember what it's like to be loved without conditions. God's love for us is not like the love we see in the world. God does not judge, punish or reward us. God loves us no matter what, and our soul seeks to be a demonstration of that unconditional love.

There are really just two primary emotions: love and fear. For love to exist, the opposite must exist, and fear is the antithesis of love. Every mortal thought and action is based in either fear or love, and we've been given free will over which of the two we choose. Love is really all there is: only love is real. Everything else is an illusion the mortal mind has created. Although fear is a jail cell that feels very real, the things we're afraid of -the overdue bill or the job that's in jeopardy-are things we made up. Fear dwells in darker, lower realms, and the energy of fear powerfully draws the circumstances to us that we feel most fearful of, so what we fear is what will torment us.

Hopelessness, anger, and disillusionment are all forms of fear. Fear's voice is the most unrelenting, and the mind loves the sound of fear's voice. Each and every emotion is merely an expression of or the absence of love. The mismanagement of our emotions keeps us from our dreams, and fear is, by far, the worst. We bring fear upon ourselves. We've created a very fearful reality for ourselves. We indulge in fearful feelings until we're left paralyzed and stop taking risks. We stop playing. Life becomes serious and joy goes missing. Abundance has no way of finding us when fear stands guard at the door.

The human mind's purpose is to create fear. The soul's purpose is to break through that fear. Anything negative we experience in life, financial nightmares included, occurs in the absence of love. Without love, our lives crumble. We crumble. Fear exposes where our barriers are to love. Our mission is to remove the barriers. Love is very sacred ground. It turns shadows into light. Love defies fear; and fear cannot exist when love is present. Love will always redeem us. It is the reason for our existence.

In reality, everything is within; the outer experience is just a projection of the contents of the mind. How often do we say, *"I'm afraid to..."* or *"I fear that..."* Our words are creative forces, so whatever we say we're afraid of we will experience. Fear and anger are also powerful creative forces, as are love and joy. Which do you choose to create with? The circumstances surrounding your finances are the projections of the fear that is within you-the anger, the jealousy, the lack of self-love-everything that is toxic within your mind. *"Am I good enough? Could I have done better? Do they really like me?"* These are the private questions that follow us.

We talk to ourselves constantly saying things like, *"I'm stupid, I'm bad, I'm a loser,"* or *"I'll never be able to do anything with my life."* No one abuses us more than we abuse ourselves. We don't accept and love ourselves, and believe we aren't lovable and aren't worthy of kindness and respect. We carry so much shame and guilt within and have such a false image of perfection. We believe we don't measure up to anyone else's ideals, so we do harm to our physical bodies to punish ourselves for not being what we want to be or feel we should be.

The feeling of love *is* God, and the power of love is alive in you. It is your heart. When your heart is open, you become the conduit for the greatest forces of life. You become the great ruler of your own kingdom. Reign mightily with love throughout your vast and beautiful empire and all things are possible-peace of mind, joy, and abundance galore. When you feel the power of love, it resonates through your heart. And when the force of love pours through your heart, the miraculous occurs.

We came willingly into this life to embrace the adventures, to embrace the choice of fulfilling on our soul's every desire. Forgetting that this is our soul's journey is part of the classroom; each life experience is a class in which we have chosen to enroll. We are on an eternal journey. It is the reason for our being. We cannot get it wrong, and there are no mistakes. Shame is the darkness that stands on the opposite side of God. We must know the darkness to know the light. Fear exists in the absence of self-love, and it's held you prisoner for far too long. The time has come for all self-hatred, shame, and guilt to end. They existed so you could discover your greatness by knowing smallness. You are not separate from God. God is inside of you, so wake up! Own your bigness and love yourself! To know and see yourself as worthy of love is the formula for becoming a prosperity powerhouse. It gifts you with the graceful capacity to fly.

Having a high vibration of self love and a love of others, you can manifest almost instantly, so become unreasonably loving in the face of no agreement. Dreams do come true and all things are possible, but when you close your eyes to love, you cast away all possibility for any dream to come into fruition. The ultimate wisdom is in knowing that love carries such tremendous power; power in its highest form. It smacks of magic. And not just any magic, but the most powerful magic of all. You cannot possibly hold the love God has for you, so letting it run through you is the only way to receive it. The more love you radiate from within, the sooner you reach the tipping point of radically shifting your level of prosperity. You no longer have to stagger and collapse to the floor the next time you're in a house of sadness. No, no, no. All you must do is allow your big, beautiful and generous heart of love to beat forth, its pulse amplifying, magnifying, multiplying, and extending outward to swiftly usher love, light, and untold blessings into the situation.

If you're wondering how to operate from love in life, it is by way of gratitude. Gratitude is the energy that bridges you to the love that you are. Gratitude *is* love; it is unconditional love. You can use the power of love to bless, transform, uplift, and dissolve every iniquity. Love is the strongest emotion of the human soul, bringing forth such magnificent power that can transform even the most seemingly impossible circumstances. Any situation bred in fear can be altered when you allow the resonance of love to burst forth to do its magnificent work. When you shift into the heart and allow the power of love to flood through, everything is brought into the light and dissolved. Call to mind whatever it is that is causing you anxiety or fear, and use the magnetic power of an open heart to deliberately invoke exquisite feelings of love. In your mind's eye, extend this beautiful loving energy outward to the circumstance and to each person involved. Bless each individual, see him or her surrounded in beautiful white light, and surrender the situation to God, releasing any attachment to the outcome. When the power of love is called upon, you can expect a pleasant and surprising outcome to a situation that initially caused fear, doubt, and suffering.

Heaven is not outside of you. Heaven exists in a state of love. Love is the flame that ignites the soul. It is the life force alive within, and it is the glory of your heart. Claim it. Not in some abstract way, but as part of your daily experience. You are the most magnificent, the most remarkable being God created. If you allowed yourself to remember this, you would never again experience fear.

The snares and rebuffs that once threw you off balance no longer stop you. Your natural-born ability to love will have you burning to climb over the next obstacle that appears. Practice this every bloomin' moment you can. I've got a proposition for you: try out the 51 Percent Rule with your love power. For the next week, take on beaming with love, radiating it outward, and slathering everyone and everything with such infectious love for at little more than half the day, and expect a twilight world filled with miracles to burst forth. Now go for it! Great changes take place from such a brilliant choice. Get your love on, hunny pie. Go on. Give it a try.

You pay homage to your own connection once you claim your divinity and become the full expression of the joyful soul you were created to be. Each moment you allow yourself to mosey along the paths of joy and love, opportunities for greater joy, bigger love, and unlimited abundance are given. Unleash the fullness of who you are. You'll become magnetic to people and circumstances aligned with the same energy. Radiate the pure energy of love and everyone will want to be near you. God, himself, will wonder how He created something so perfect.

Your little mortal mind cannot grasp your cosmic capabilities, unlimited in scope. The energy of love is washing over you now. The horizon looms large, wide under the blue sky. And for you, my dear, the vista is unlimited. Your destiny is at hand, always. You possess characteristics so transcendent and sublime they elude classification. You are especially gorgeous today. Allow yourself to indulge in the adventure. You have the look duels are fought for…and won. Hubba, hubba. Kiss, kiss.

Feelings of profound joy and happiness are constant for me.

> "You don't have to go looking for love when it's where you come from."
> **-Werner Erhard**

> "I found that when you start thinking and saying what you really want then your mind automatically shifts and pulls you in that direction. And sometimes it can be that simple, just a little twist in vocabulary that illustrates your attitude and philosophy."
> **- Jim Rohn**

I now easily and effortlessly earn over $_____ each year.

TODAY'S GOALS

Tired of living below your potential? Want bigger and better things? How about achieving your every dream? Then get serious about your goal setting, sweetheart.
It's the key to cutting-edge performance.

_____   _____
_____   _____
_____   _____
_____   _____
_____   _____

THINGS FOR WHICH I'M GRATEFUL

Love is powerful creative energy. Dare to unearth the love within every person and everything. Having the courage to make that your focus and your entire life will alter. Big time. I promise.

_____   _____
_____   _____
_____   _____

AFFIRMATIONS
Incredible things happen to me every single day.

_____
_____
_____
_____
_____
_____
_____
_____
_____
_____
_____

Day 22 - You Are the Light.

"The true enemy is inside. The maker of trouble, the source of all our suffering, the destroyer of our joy, and the destroyer of our virtue is inside. It is Ego. "- Gehlik Rimoche

A life-threatening diagnosis, an end to a 20-year marriage, a tragic accident involving someone we desperately loved. It's the news we're never expecting. Must we wait to suffer a life-altering devastation to force us into making the changes that have been long overdue for years? None of us is getting out of here alive, so what are you waiting for? You've opened The Doors of Daring, and if you aren't practicing managing your mind power on a daily basis, you're waiting on the front porch and living at half-light. What's it going to take for you to begin inundating your mind with the affirmations? To use the great power of your imagination to have your every dream fulfilled? To speak your life right into physical existence?

I'm serious as a heart attack when I tell you that consistent focused effort is what gives birth to the life that's waiting for you to step into. Still you merely dabble in your efforts with this work. Let me tell you a story about a woman who merely dabbled with her mind training.

Gail was in her mid-fifties when she decided to move to a new city to start her life from scratch. She was divorced, her children now grown. For years, she worked part-time in various jobs that paid her little and had health insurance. Like most people, she barely made ends meet each month. She carried big aspirations in her heart, and moving to a bigger city was her ticket to the promise land.

Sixteen months after she'd relocated her life, she packed her things and moved back to where she was living before, broke and with her tail between her legs. A black cloud of failure loomed so fierce it made her face wince. We had a conversation the night before she left, and she cried dragon tears, sorrowing in such heavy emotions. She said she'd been repeating her affirmations "all the time", but they just didn't work for her. She repeatedly said she was a hard worker, adding that she "loved to work hard". Yet she couldn't succeed. I told Gail that her 'work hard' belief was the underlying problem of her inability to launch a new life.

In the time I knew Gail, she consistently used the word 'hard' to describe most things related to work, money, and relationships. Because she held such a deep-seated belief that life is hard, that's precisely what she experienced. While Gail was indeed brave and bold enough to relocate her life to a new city, she didn't do any advanced scouting for employment before she moved. Yes, she could have been more responsible and found a job before she moved, but there are people who do get lucky breaks, right? Not Gail. The initial joy and excitement of starting life over dissipated quickly when the endless hours of online job searching produced no results. Fear, doubt, and self-pity consumed her the more time she spent in solitude.

She began withdrawing from much social interaction. After several months, a friend helped her land a part-time job that paid $10 an hour. Having no health insurance, Gail's financial agony grew worse after a few trips to the emergency room, after a fall in a parking lot and a recurring abscess that required medical treatment. She'd been living for free with a friend who allowed her to stay until she could get on her feet. After a year passed, with no financial contribution from Gail, the relationship began to strain. Her car was in unreliable condition and a cause of significant worry for her when it got sideswiped. The bills continued to pile up. There was one breakdown after another, and Gail's emotional suffering caused her to sink lower and lower each day. Can you see how hard life is for Gail? The energy we emit draws to us the circumstances that mirror our energy, and unless we do something significantly different to shift that energy the stream of struggle will only continue.

Besides having such a deeply ingrained negative belief that life is hard, the most striking blow to Gail's geographic failure was the extreme self-loathing that caused her to shrink in life. Gail told me all she ever wanted was to be loved. She cried often and was sad most of the time, dwelling in self-pity. Not having a love-of-self only kept Gail living a hard life filled with emotional suffering, obstacles, and let downs. She didn't play like she mattered because she didn't believe she mattered. The voices of self-hatred, self-rejection, and criticism were always amplified in her head and described a body image that wasn't accurate. When she shared with me what the voices repeatedly said to her, I felt only the deepest compassion for her.

When those voices are in a never-ending dialogue they can be awfully convincing. Only we decide if what they say is true. Gail listened often enough and hung on their every word. The voices drove her to excessive exercise routines, infrequent eating, and exhaustion. Her internal dialogue told her she wasn't good enough, thin enough, or pretty enough. There's no cheese down that tunnel, yet we still venture down the tunnel-unless we intentionally choose otherwise. Gail's repeated money affirmations, mostly done on a treadmill, made no difference for her. She may have repeated them frequently, but she did nothing else to connect with her inner creative clout. Her dark emotions, left unattended eventually conquered, leaving her worse off than before.

When our focus remains on the external world, we have no access to our internal power. When we don't acknowledge the godliness within, we suffer and we stagnate. Everything gets sorted out when we allow the mind to quiet. Once we quiet the mind and tap into our heart, we can experience the wisdom, abundance, love, joy and peace that is that is available in unlimited supply. In the silence, we venture deep inside ourselves and unravel the soul. In the silence, we remember we *are* the light waiting to be released to create our own version of heaven on earth. We can't create anything good for ourselves when we're convinced there's nothing good about ourselves. Self-hatred is powerful creative energy. Gail's self-hatred was like a dense fog that blocked any ounce of goodness from freely entering her experience. It was impossible for her to be a catalyst for prosperity- her focus was always outward instead of inward.

There's a little bit of Gail in all of us. We stop trying when things don't go our way, especially when adversity steps in. We give up intentionally creating our lives and shift to merely surviving our circumstances. We live like we're lost souls, waiting for someone or something to come along and save the day. No one is coming. Nothing can save you. You must save yourself.

You cannot just snap your fingers (not yet anyway) and suddenly prosperity appears. It takes conscious effort on an on-going basis to transcend your self-imposed limitations. You've forgotten you were granted free will and the freedom to choose your life to be any way you want it to be. You can be sad, happy, rich, or poor. You choose it all. You can create anything at anytime. You were born out of a vast ocean of possibilities and can tap into endless possibilities each time you swim in the waters of thought.Your power as a creator is within you always. If you could only remember how powerful you are in creating your life-your reality-you'd make different choices.

You'd manage your emotions and where you placed your focus. You'd be more intentional with your mind training.

The shame you feel must stop. It no longer serves a purpose. Simply remember who you are and why you are here. You're on the cusp of a spiritual awakening. Today is the beginning of the rest of your life. There's a reason you are here. You are God experiencing himself through your body, emotions, and thoughts. Once you understand this, the shame you carry dissolves. You are a divine spiritual being living in a human body for just a few decades. You are enough. Do you understand that? Once you know you're enough exactly as you are, you become kinder, gentler, and more loving.

Self-love is what's missing in most of us. We bawl our eyes out wanting to be heard, loved, and accepted. The love we crave isn't outside of us. It's within us. The ability to love ourselves is the greatest gift, yet most of us have forgotten this. Instead we choose to create fear and panic, and we induce others to join us. Within love lies everything we need to know, be, or do. It's always been there. We simply need to tap into it. We become overly preoccupied with our little 'imperfections', yet we are perfect just as we are.

How much do you love yourself? What is it that stops you from fully accepting yourself? Stand in front of a mirror, look into your eyes and say, *"I love and approve of myself just the way I am."* Begin to love *you*. Love every one of your flaws, inequities, and magnificent beauty equally. Know in that moment you can realize the full love of yourself, if you chose it. Having such a profound inner love as a tapped resource, you can create anything you want. Anything! There is so much love here for you and so much love around you. You need only decide to look for it to infuse your world with the beauty of what you long for most.

The force of love is the strongest force that exists. You are beautifully human with tears. Your capacity to love is endless. Don't allow fear to overpower you. Allow love to overpower you- especially love -of-self. Human beings don't share their love freely most of the time. We share our love with conditions and give love only with the intention of getting love back. But not you, you beautiful prosperity master. You are the light! You don't ask for love. *You just give it.* Pour love from your heart and do so with reckless abandon. Try it out. Watch what happens. Abundance will come. Got it? Now hop to it.

I love and approve of myself exactly as I am.

> "It may be, dear friend, that you have been trying too hard in a personal way and have not taken time to relax, to let go, and realize that 'I am in the Father, and the Father in me.' Sometimes our attention becomes so engrossed in the things we are trying to do that we forget to unify ourselves consciously with the source of our being."
> **-Myrtle Fillmore**

I now easily and effortlessly earn over $_____ each year.

Everything I touch turns to gold.

TODAY'S GOALS

You are extraordinary, so be that everywhere you go. Be intentional in every single corner of your life: your finances, physical appearance, health, mind training, and relationships. What can you do today to expand your wings even further?

THINGS FOR WHICH I'M GRATEFUL

"Love one another and help others to rise to the higher levels, simply by pouring out love. Love is infectious and the greatest healing energy."
-*Sai Baba*

AFFIRMATIONS

You have the power.

Day 23 - I've Got that Joy, Joy, Joy, Joy Down in My Heart!

"Joy does not simply happen to us. We have to choose joy and keep choosing it every day. It is a choice based on the knowledge that we belong to God and have found in God our refuge and our safety and that nothing, not even death, can take God away from us. Joy is the experience of knowing that you are unconditionally loved and that nothing--sickness, failure, emotional distress, oppression, war, or even death--can take that love away." -Henri Nouwen

Living average days amidst a painful pattern of average weeks, we reached a point where we stalled. There's been little forward movement, and now that we're thinking of it, it feels like we've been stalled longer than memory serves. Inspiration has slipped beneath the thick skin of our thick skin. The life we want seems impossible to have, so far out of reach. We feel broken in so many, many ways. Life was not intended to be hard. We were never intended to suffer, yet how bloody difficult the journey has turned out to be. Here's a news flash: You've been settling for an average life.

Consider this your pre-magnificent stage. The best is yet to come. It is only when you shine your glorious light that magnificence arises where nothing stood before. The reward and promise of your journey is magnificent. As a divine creation of God, your birthright is all the love, abundance and joy the universe has to offer. It is only when you believe otherwise that suffering consumes you. You get to choose whether you take the journey in tears, or with love in your heart and unbridled joy radiating from your soul. Yet we still choose to suffer, and suffering only keeps prosperity at bay. It's time to make drastically different choices.

Challenges are meant to inspire us, and difficulties are the lessons from which to learn. We have forgotten who we are. The time to remember is now. Once we remember, the door opens. When we suffer with negative emotions, amnesia sets in and the door closes. The more joy we experience in this physical lifetime, the more we remember who we really are. Joy is not the only key to remembering who we really are; joy *is* who we really are. At the level of our soul, we came here for one simple reason: to experience joy by exercising our divine power to create absolutely anything we want. Our soul is *always* in a state of eternal bliss, eternal joy. This is our natural way of being.

Sadly, our lives have become devoid of joy. We yearn for the rewarding, high-paying job that leaves every inch of us fulfilled, but we stopped believing in Fate after resignation arrived. It destroyed hope. We trusted that Dr. Phil would make everything all right and we went straight back to watching TV. If offends the heavens when we linger in situations that don't bring us joy. We remain in joyless relationships, jobs, or conditions that mute our holiness. Anytime we're feeling a negative emotion, we are in that very moment disconnected from our soul. We have forgotten who we really are, and the door closes once again

Scarcity perception and joylessness go hand-in-hand, my friend. Whatever we emote, returns to us. Negative energy draws to us negative circumstances and negative people to reflect our negative way of being. Angry people are magnetically drawn to angry people. When we are in such a nasty energetic space, the statement we declare to the universe is, "Hey there, unlimited universe. How you doin'? Please send me more of the people, circumstances, and things that match the way I'm strongly feeling in this very minute of life, OK? Thanks, doll." Then the car breaks down, the check bounces, and our job is in jeopardy again.

We're either choosing joy or we're choosing suffering. We choose it all. We resist doing what is most joyful because we are enslaved by the thought forms that tell us we must work hard at joyless occupations. Negative emotions are debilitating to the creation process, and if we aren't mindful, our emotions snare us into joyless situations. We have settled for what passes for 'joy' in life. We remain in situations or relationships that are far from being joyful, and yet we do nothing about it.

Consider that our deep seated belief that we don't deserve joy may be the reason we do nothing to change our negative circumstances. By staying in the job or relationship where we feel undervalued and unappreciated, we affirm that we are not worthy of anything better. We are, in effect, undervaluing and under-appreciating ourselves. Others are simply mirroring this to us.

We will only have true joy in life when we focus on allowing it. It certainly behooves us to pay attention to what we're paying attention to. When we listen to the daily news, we're paying attention to what most of the world is focusing on: scarcity, crime, war, and struggle. And how does this make us feel? Certainly not joyful. We are not obligated to do anything that does not bring us joy, and we certainly aren't duty bound to spend time with those who drain our energy, dishonor, or disrespect us. Our peer group is something we get to choose. Choosing to surround ourselves with big dreamers and daft creators just like us promotes our own excellence.

If it has been a while since you have had a good laugh, you really should change that. Humor is good for the soul, good for our wellbeing, and priceless for our emotional state of mind. There's something intrinsically spiritual in laughter. The human mind is so extraordinarily powerful it can alter our DNA. When you laugh hard, your whole body laughs. Each atom-each cell participates in it. It stimulates the immune system and burns calories. Norman Cousins is well known for curing his cancer using the great power of his mind and the healing power of laughter. With the determination that perhaps only a person facing a death sentence can muster, Cousins made laughter the powerful medicine that put his cancer into remission. He discovered was that five minutes of hard belly laughing relieved his intense physical pain for several hours, and allowed him to sleep peacefully.

What's the difference between laughing about something and crying over it? Attitude, sweetie darling. Which would you rather do? Laughter suspends sorrow, fear, and anger, allowing us to be as carefree as kids. It affords us the ability to shift into our hearts and experience joy, even when we've become emotionally crippled. It's cathartic, generating transcendence, reverence, joy, passion and love. When we're weepy, overcome with worry, and squeezed by the stress of our circumstances, we can laugh if off! And not just giggling or chuckling. The kind of laughter that can't be contained or we'd implode. Laughing 'till your face hurts. Such squeals of delight and shrieks of elation leave a profound residue of joy. Oh. Em. Gee.

We're at the mercy of the mortal mind, and if we don't run it, it runs us. Hell and heaven are within us. They are neighbors in the mind. One moment you're in heaven, the next moment you're in hell. It goes on in this manner continuously. Not controlling the mind is what causes us to jump from one yard to the next. When the mind is in control, we live life unconsciously and stay in hell the majority of the time. Our peace of mind is sporadic and left to chance. When we are intentional with our thoughts and emotions, we live life consciously and hang out mostly in heaven. Our attitude, our state of mind, and how we're feeling is what determines in which yard we play. Our internal state is what there is to be intentional with. The more often we are free of the heavy emotional baggage we lug around, the easier it is to access joy. When we are joyful far more often than we are fearful or angry, joy becomes so integrated, so consolidated, that we never lose it. There is no more hell for us. *Please listen carefully: joy will set you free from the suffering.* That's why laughter is so very special.

We have access to mansions of joy when we are lifted above the chatter that kicks around in our craniums. A good dose of laughter emboldens us in times of defeat, and elevates us to higher-frequency energy levels. Higher frequency energy levels unleash our creative powers. There's nothing we can't create when our energy levels are overflowing.

Oh, the seriousness of it all! Sometimes we get all sad pants and need a good cry to release the hurt, pain, or humiliation we experience as the result of a not-so-good situation. Go ahead, let it rip. Cry it out, baby. The moment you are blissful, the mind disappears. The more often you practice this, the more ingrained joy becomes. Being consistently joyful is beyond breathtakingly awesome. It draws abundance to you, my Charming Dodo, so excel in the deliberate practice of it.

Need some suggestions as to how to bubble up with joy on a regular basis? Consider these:

Some good over-the-top hardy laughter catapults you right up to cloud nine. This is the cloud where all the action is. Nothing clears out the emotional crud faster than watching funny movies. Here's your radical, visionary plan: Channel your inner Will Ferrell and Tina Fey and develop that sense of humor of yours. Have fun with abundance and abundance will most certainly have fun with you. I invite you to become a hardcore prankster. (Heh. Heh.) Play some hella tricks on the peeps you know. Nothing that would cause them bodily harm, of course, but something that shakes things up a bit. Go toilet paper a friend's house at midnight or something. Trust me. This is going to be great. You'll laugh all the way to bank.

Joy is potent energy in manifestation's laboratory. Each and every time you allow yourself to move along the path of joy, your energy field is wide open and flowing. This is the path of least resistance, so take it. Deliberately feel profound joy throughout the day. Make this your primary goal, and I assure you, your life will change.

Want to have an un-average day of implausible prosperity making? Allow joy to radiate from every molecule of your body. Become a constant expression of joy and bliss and fly your heart out like a kite. Joyful is what you are meant to be. It's been negotiated into your soul contract. Radiate joy in all directions, believing in the magic that occurs because of it. You're now vigilant in the craft of it. Yep. Roger that! You're a true-blue joy spreader. There's no time to delay. You have an overflow of joy to spread all over God's green globe.

There's a playful spiritual being inside all of us. Go where the sun shines brightest and let yours out to play. Follow that bliss and you'll never lose. You are the light, keeper of the universe through your heart and love. Whatever feels joyful is Spirit simply reminding you of who you really are. Chokes me up every time. Now get out there and shake your tail feathers and show 'em what you're made of. You've got this manifestation stuff handled. You're so enthusiastic, you can't sit. And you are totally into forgiveness too. Does it get any better than this?! I think not. Your life just keeps getting better and better. Oh go on....

I now easily and effortlessly earn over $_____each year.

TODAY'S GOALS

What will you accomplish today? Who will you be today that will make a difference?
Be the cause in the matter of your own life.

_____   _____
_____   _____
_____   _____
_____   _____
_____   _____

THINGS FOR WHICH I'M GRATEFUL

Wonderful things always happen for me. I am always grateful.

_____   _____
_____   _____
_____   _____

AFFIRMATIONS

When the going gets a little tough, write your affirmations. They will always pull you forward.

_____
_____
_____
_____
_____
_____
_____
_____
_____
_____
_____
_____

Day 24 - Childlike Wonder

"If I had influence with the good fairy who is supposed to preside over the christening of all children, I should ask that her gift to each child in the world be a sense of wonder so indestructible that it would last throughout life." -Rachel Carson

Remember when you thought you could fly with fairies, swing from tall trees in overgrown jungles, carry on secret conversations with animals, live in enchanted castles by the sea, and blow luminous bubbles all the way up to heaven? Remember that? Remember being pushed on a swing real fast, and when you jumped off it felt like you were flying for a half a second? Remember that? You'd catch lightening bugs on hot summer nights and stay up late telling such scary ghost stories you swore you were gonna pee your pants. Remember that? Huh? Remember that?

Beaming smiles, infectious laughter, endless energy, curiosity, imagination, creativity, and wonder- these are all the wonderful characteristics of a child. It may take something for you to recall what it was like to be a child when the world was chock full of wonder. Or maybe not.

Children know the magical power of their imaginations, and they use it to conjure up dreamy rich fantasy worlds where the wisdom of fairy tales sparkles through. As children, there was innate possibility and curiosity in absolutely everything we did. We could create anything in our imaginations, like castles and spaceships, driftwood forts, mud pies, flying blue pigs with yellow wings, pink unicorns, and purple horses. There were no boundaries. No limits. It was a beautiful world where anything could happen and anything was possible.

When asked as children what we wanted to be when we grew up, we never once shouted from the sand box, *"When I grow up, I want to be unemployed, bankrupt, broke and evicted from my home!! It'll be sooooo much fun being pissed off all the time living through the financial hell I'm going to create for myself!! Yaaaaaaaay!"* No, we never clung to such nightmarish aspirations. We were pure as snow, and believed absolutely anything was possible, even flying. But as grownups, we've had our fair share of the trauma brought on by the nightmares of our own mis-creations. We didn't dream of a life that would be this chaotic and untidy. No, my dear. We did not.

Don't you look at me in that tone of voice! You're fried, frazzled and burned out. Pack your bags. Load the dishwasher. Water the plants. And runnnnnnnnn to the nearest playground!

There's boldness, a spark, when we allow childlike play and wonder to fill our hearts. Joy is our birthright, and love is what we're born with. We were created to love and be loved, and the love within us is intended to extend outward.

Children have wild and creative imaginations, and they're filled with pure love and joy. They radiate it. We feel lighter and more playful in their presence. *They remind us of who we were created to be.* Our pets belong in the elite group of happy-go-lucky-joy-spreaders, too. I swear my beagle frequently talks to fairies. She's always in high spirits, never having had one bad day, hour, minute, or even a second for that matter. And her joy expands over to me. I'm the providential beneficiary of her interaction with those fairies who giggle and play with her when I leave the house, and I'm not complaining about it one bit. No siree. What a good little beagle she is.

Love and joy are potent, wildly creative forces. They are the fuel for our magic wands of thought, emotion and imagination. We're being intentional with the potent powers of love and joy lately, knowing full well these are the two best feelings in the world that draw magnificent abundance.

Now let's take a look at wonder, shall we? Wonder is wonderful thing. We're going to get very familiar with wonder, since it's supremely useful in the creation process.

When something beautiful, extraordinary, and unexpected occurs, we experience wonder. As we witness the unfolding of a miracle, it is wonder that apprehends us. As we stand in awe of something marvelous, wonder delightfully bubbles to the surface. It shatters the ordinary and transforms it into the miraculous. It is here where our tender souls sigh. When my boys were small, I found such sustenance in the exquisite wonder that would surround me as I watched them sleep peacefully. I'd get so lost in the experience that an hour would pass though it seemed like just minutes.

When we look at something with such curiosity, it is as though it were the first time we've seen it, and we are overtaken with wonder. Children reside in a realm of wonder. It is here where curiosity reigns. Children are profoundly curious. The world is still so new to them; each day is gifted with new discoveries, new possibilities, and plenty of new adventures. We've seen the look often enough. A child experiences something for the first time, and the awe is so overwhelming that he actually swims in it. The experience of it is so mesmerizing that his jaw drops open, and his eyes become fixed on whatever it is that's so captivating. When we are struck with wonder, the very experience of it envelops us to the extent that we are rendered speechless.

We sure did fall a lot as children. We scraped our knees, cried it out and started playing again. Our return to joy was almost immediate. We could do this as adults too if we'd just stop pouting all the time. We act like heathens when we walk around crying our brains out like someone has died. *Come on.* Adaptability is being willing to follow our own paths and remain stable in unchartered territory. No pouting allowed.

We're as tame as trees trying to be such good boys and girls. Yet the mother hen of doubt, dread, and fear always seems to interfere just when things start getting good for us, and life ends up knocking us around again. Egads. We've really forgotten how powerful and magical we are. We're at the intersection of hope and bliss, and if we allow light and love to illumine our path, we would never get lost again.

We'd like bigger and better moods these days, and more often, please. So how can we use wonder to make manifest our wishes and dreams? Here's how: concern and worry cannot exist in the presence of wonder. Aha! When we are struck with wonder, we are elevated high above the lion's roar of turmoil and confusion that distracts us, and our busy minds are wiped clean of the muddle of everyday concerns. This is useful information! We can't create much of anything when our minds are off running the next race. If we allow wonder to quiet the mind, we are then primed to make magic. For creative geniuses like us, there is no limit to what we can create standing in a state of wonder.

We can accomplish great things for mankind and ourselves when we flood our hearts with childlike wonder, joy, and love. The more often we do, the lighter we become. Invoke wonder as often as you can. Be intentional about it and practice every day. Allowing supreme goodness to penetrate your experience makes for a very happy heart.

Here's a goodie. Try this: stand tall, close your eyes, and begin taking a few slow, deep breaths. Opens your arms wide and call forth the energy of love, joy, and prosperity, allowing it to flow freely to you and through you. Feel the intoxicating energy being drawn to you. Bathe your soul in this beautiful experience for a minute or two. What you're doing is accelerating the delivery of abundance. This is fact. Believe it.

Today, ask yourself, *"I wonder what great things will come my way today?"* Then go about your day and create with joy, create with love, and create with a child-like sense of wonder. Don't be such a rule follower. Explore, experiment, play, and dance in the rain the next time the heavens water the earth. Be scared and do the thing you're afraid to do anyway. That's the definition of courage. And know this: Absolutely nothing can prevail over love. So don't be covert with wonder, joy, and love, my friend. Joy and wonder will always redeem you when the going gets tough. Make an about-face to love. It's already within you. You simply need to let it out.

It's an anything-can-happen Sunday, Monday, Tuesday, *any*-day afternoon, so hold on to your britches! (Please, try not to make a scene.) As often as you can, allow a state of dreamy carefree wonder and uninhibited curiosity to rule the day. You'll find the wisdom of the fairy queens there. To be a child is to believe in fairies, angel dust, striped unicorns, and Santa Claus; to believe in love; to believe in turning pumpkins into carriages and mice into horses. Never again forget what every child knows: that you have your very own fairy godmother deep within your soul. Learn how to have fun again. I dare you; I double dare you. Now go play or I'm gonna tell on you!

I dream big.

I am now living happily ever after.

I am my own special brand of greatness. 'Dat's right. I'm bad.

> "You can understand and relate to most people better if you look at them-no matter how old or impressive they may be-as if they are children. For most of us never really grow up or mature all that much-we simply grow taller. O, to be sure, we laugh less and play less and wear uncomfortable disguises like adults, but beneath the costume is the child we always are, whose needs are simple, whose daily life is still best described by fairy tales."
> **-Leo Rosten**

I easily and effortlessly earn over $_____**each year.**

TODAY'S GOALS

Sift, sort, and simplify. Bring order to your home. By doing so, you bring order to your mind. Is there one small action that you can complete today to coax your dreams into fruition? Then do that.

THINGS FOR WHICH I'M GRATEFUL

I am perfect, whole, and complete. Yowza!

AFFIRMATIONS

All your real advancements must come from your individual effort. Positively visualize your life of abundance and *feel it as if it's already true.*

Day 25 - Concentration Skills: Master This and You Can Create Absolutely Anything

"Fairy Tales are more than true; not because they tell us that dragons exist, but because they tell us that dragons can be beaten." -G. K. Chesterton

Lurking in shadowy darkness, they circle us like prey. They keep our dreams at bay, depriving us of our joy, our peace of mind, and our capacity to experience true contentment. Each one of us has had a fire-breathing dragon at our door at one time or another. The darkest, most ravenous dragons are the concerns, the worries, the tense financial woes we've inadvertently spent a lifetime cultivating, feeding, and nurturing. Our dragons are the ruthless bill collectors, the repeatedly overdrawn checking account, and the small fortune in fees we must pay as result.

We close our eyes against the sun, keeping constant nerve-wrecking watch, exhausting all of our emotional energy reacting and defending against the next dragon lurking in the darkness. But knowing how to bravely slay each evil dragon provides us access to the kingdom of financial ecstasy. Our potential is limitless-we're the only ones who put a lid on it.

You've been on the lookout for your very own rainbow with two pots of gold, please. You pray to win the lottery. Heck, you're this close to running off to join the next circus that comes to town to avoid having to endure one more day of the vice grip of financial burden. Right now, know that all is well. You're emerging from the fog of battle, and you'll be better than you ever thought possible.

We do too much and live too little. Multi-tasking: friend or foe? We've become proud and giddy masters of multi-tasking, haven't we? We're so busy being busy that we're unable to fully concentrate on much of anything. Juggling numerous tasks simultaneously without giving concentrated thought to any one of the tasks we're engaged in certainly gets things accomplished, but we're not really creating anything new. Most of the time, our thoughts are fragmented, moving wildly in directions of which we have no control. Without concentration, our lives become little more than an existence ruled by the subconscious. We're simply "doing". There's little time for just "being", which allows us to tap into the internal worlds that purify our mental and emotional energy.

The common denominator in those who struggle financially is that they've never developed or mastered the skill of thought concentration-positive thought concentration-in the area of money. I have a news flash for you: anyone who struggles financially hasn't practiced concentrating on prosperity. Otherwise they would experience prosperity. Being unable to concentrate well and control the mind puts us at grave risk for a life of struggle and unhappiness. This is precisely how we end up living a life by default. To be successful in creating anything, we must fully concentrate our entire thought upon the very thing we want to produce.

We all know those who give everything they've got to just "getting by," and as a result, they do just that. No shit. These folks live at half-throttle. I wonder what would be the result if instead they gave everything they had by blowing it out of the water and knocking it out of the ballpark? These half-throttlers would have fewer monsters under their beds if they simply concentrated their efforts at every at bat they had to actually produce the things in life that made their hearts sing and their spirits fly.

Those who dwell in the realm of negativity develop abstraction of the mind. Their ability to concentrate hasn't been developed. We know those who are consistently and malignantly negative. We dread being with them since they suck the life force right out of us. Instead, they perpetuate their financial struggles by repeatedly talking about them. They talk incessantly on topics of absolutely no importance. In fact, they talk simply for the sake of talking. They watch a lot of TV. They complain a great deal. They have plenty of great ideas but never seem to take action because they don't spend enough time concentrating on any one of them. Their minds are off running a race, darting from one thought to the next. Lots of us have initiative, but instead of concentrating it into one direction, we diffuse it through several, thereby dissipating it to such an extent that the original idea gets lost…and we're off creating the next great idea. If we scatter our energies to the four winds, we will never achieve consistent prosperity in life.

Mental discipline is absolutely imperative in the prosperity manifestation process, and the only way to master mental discipline is through daily practice. Catch my drift? As a child, you didn't learn how to ride a bike without first practicing. You started with training wheels, and when you were ready to have the training wheels removed, someone ran alongside holding you steady on the bike while you practiced concentrating on finding balance. Then it happened. You learned balance all on your own, and your world was never the same.

It is the same with mastering your mind power. The outcome will always be inexplicably potent once we know how to harness it. Developing a new money mindset takes practice and concentrated effort. In order to develop new financial thought habits that foster a new financial belief system, we must practice concentrating on new thoughts until they become automatic. It is in the practicing that we are fully concentrating.

The effort in playing a musical instrument is 90% mental and 10% physical. It is the same with your prosperity training. An accomplished pianist was not born an accomplished pianist. He first had the desire to play the piano, so he began taking piano lessons. In learning how to play the piano, the mind tells the fingers what to do, not the other way around. We can practice playing the piano for an hour, and in that hour accomplish nothing if we are not fully concentrating on the entire piece of music, every inch of it, every fingering, every dynamic, every articulation. The power of our focus is everything. What we place our attention upon, we amplify. It is that simple… nothing else.

Somewhere in Time is a time-spanning love story that I tortured myself with during one of my many nights of despair. Feeling wimpy, lonely and hopeless, I watched Robert Collier, a contemporary playwright, played by Christopher Reeve, fall deeply in love with Elise McKenna. While staying at the Grand Hotel on Mackinac Island, Robert sees a portrait of Elise, a beautiful stage actress who had performed there in 1912. He is so enchanted with the beautiful Elise that he becomes obsessed with the idea of traveling back to 1912 to meet her. It just so happens that Robert's old college professor, Dr. Gerard Finney, wrote a book on time travel, and he tells Richard that he briefly time traveled to 1571 using the power of self-suggestion. To accomplish this through self-hypnosis, Dr. Finney tells Richard that all objects from the present time period must be removed to trick the mind into believing that it now exists in the past.

Richard ventures off to buy an early 20th century suit and some vintage coins. Dressed in the vintage suit, he removes all modern objects from his hotel room and attempts to will himself into the year 1912 using tape-recorded suggestions, but fails miserably. Rummaging through the hotel's attic, Richard finds an old guest book from 1912 with his signature in it and realizes that he will eventually succeed at his quest to time travel to meet Elise. Game on. Richard delves deep into the task again and hypnotizes himself using the tape recorder suggestions; it's unwavering faith that finally propels his journey back through time. The self-hypnosis carries him off to a deep sleep, and he awakens to the sound of whinnying horses on June 27, 1912, and the love affair begins.

Time traveling via self-hypnosis may not be your cup of tea, but you'll soon find that while doing this work, something phenomenal happens. Boldness, magic and providence begin to appear to aid you in your quest. I've experienced this firsthand so often that I now know the more I allow Spirit to move through me using my talents and my gifts, a divine gifting takes place. Everything I need appears at precisely the perfect time in the perfect form, and it gives me goose bumps every single time.

I had never been savvy in the art of concentration. I certainly wasn't born with the skill, and I never learned how to cultivate it. My untamed thoughts always moved quickly and without direction, never allowing me to complete tasks of importance. Learning how to concentrate by fully placing my attention on what I wanted to occur for me was absolutely essential in my financial transformation. I knew this, and yet I struggled, especially with my visualizations. A few days after watching that sappy love story, something synchronous happened. The summer catalog from a community college arrived in the mail. A two week course in hypnosis was being offered for $20. I could hear angels whispering to my soul. I profoundly felt their direction. I knew I was being guided, supported, and lifted up. No longer did I feel like I was rotting in the fields. I felt sanctioned to take my life on in a way I'd never thought possible, so I took the class and drastically improved my concentration skills. It was another piece to the puzzle, a tool I added to my ever-expanding tool belt. I was now able to focus like a laser on creating prosperity.

Where we place our time, energy, and focus determines the reality in which we live. We continue to worry about our financial shortcomings, and more of the same financial shortcomings occur. The thoughts we think either make us happy or they make us unhappy. If the thoughts we're thinking make us happy, then we should continue thinking those happy thoughts. But if they are not happy thoughts, if they are not producing joyful emotions, we have chosen a negative habit of thought. Let's decide instead to choose a different thought at that moment. In doing so, we will shine. We powerfully create our every experience, and our emotions are the driving force. The Law of Attraction always, always, always says 'yes' and delivers in tangible form that which is a vibrational match to our emotions.

This much I know: the single most valuable skill in creating abundance is to concentrate and focus your attention on abundance. You're lost without it. This crucial tool will change the quality of your life. I promise. Go ahead, say it: *"But I don't wanna."* Listen up, doll. If we don't expand ourselves, we stagnate. And until we do, we will remain stifled. We've been dissociated from our fundamental knowledge. We have gone unconscious and forgotten we had mystical keys to the treasure chest chock full of unlimited possibilities. God gifted us with powers that grow exponentially once we become proficient with concentration. Our wizardry skills will multiply once we morph into the creative masters we were born to be. Mastering concentration is the miracle we've been waiting for.

Once you learn how to concentrate your mind on prosperity, you can get absolutely anything you want-any income, any house, any car, anything. Join the forces of mind, body and spirit, and your every wish is granted.

There is great wisdom and power within you. Yes, you. Practice the laws within this book and *everything* is possible. Make yourself a promise. Give the tools a fair chance. They will help you find your way. Do the daily work outlined here, and the experience of the journey is enhanced manifold. Today, be mindful of every single task you're engaged in. Allow yourself to be fully present in whatever it is you're doing and concentrate your focus there. If your mind begins to wander, and it will, gently call it back to the task at hand.

Can you begin to glimpse how powerful you are? Very soon, you'll wave one of your mighty wands, recite a pretty little spell, and effect a very magical creation into existence. Abracadabra! Prosperity is on the horizon!

What could frost my cake more than appreciating the life I'm living right now?!

I believe in miracles of every kind.

"Cleanse your mind with the soap of concentration, and wash it with the water of meditation."
-**Sri Ramana Maharshi**

"It is felt that a disciplined mind leads to happiness and an undisciplined mind leads to suffering..."
- **Dalai Lama**

I now easily and effortlessly earn over $_____ each year.

TODAY'S GOALS

Record all the things you'll accomplish today. This is how you create your life to look the way you want it to. You're no longer living by default. Yours is a life by design. Try something new. Take up yoga. Study French cooking. Swing on a trapeze or go sky diving, if you've always wanted to! But above all, remember to spend the time to doing your visualizations, affirmations, and managing your emotional state.

THINGS FOR WHICH I'M GRATEFUL
I am so proud of me.

AFFIRMATIONS
Affirmations set in motion exactly what you want to occur for you.
Repeat them as often as you can.

Day 26 - A Wing and a Prayer

"That prayer has great power which a person makes with all his might. It makes a sour heart sweet, a sad heart merry, a poor heart rich, a foolish heart wise, a timid heart brave, a sick heart well, a blind heart full of sight, a cold heart ardent. It draws down the great God into the little heart; it drives the hungry soul up into the fullness of God; it brings together two lovers, God and the soul, in a wondrous place where they speak much of love."
-Mechthild of Magheburg

We hurl faith and hope right out the door when we take an emotional nose dive. Thank you very much. We've been looking to the outer world for comfort, peace of mind, and our sanity, only to realize just how far off track we've wandered, but this time we're really lost. The artificial chatter is numbing. We've bloodied our knees often enough from the recurring spiritual heart attacks we suffer as we go it alone in our faithlessness.

We dwell in despair when we deny our spiritual roots. No wonder there are days we awaken to a mood so foul, one choppy negative emotion smashes into the next without reprieve. Have a little faith, will you? Faith assures us hope, respite from the many wars we have endured. Surrendering it all to God is the anchor point for our storm-tossed souls. We receive God's peace when we ask for it, and prayer, my friend, is the conduit. It is the return to hope, to tranquility and serenity. It is in prayer that we unearth our real creative power.

Once I slowed down enough to discover the moments of calm and clarity, I was gently navigated down the path of abundance, rather than being herded by yet another circumstance that sent me spinning. When I was at the brink of complete financial scarcity, I decided I would sell all the furniture in the house to get us through the summer. I had an auction first. Whatever was left I sold at our garage sale. Lots of angst and lots of drama began to emerge as our belongings were carried away. I felt a shame deeper and sadder than I had words for. On that day, I was ugly. I had lost all faith in my ability to attract any goodness. It was a pathetic malady. The empty rooms in our house yawned mockingly at me. Exhausted from the emotional nose dive I took, I began to share with God how broken I was. I shared, and shared, and shared until there was nothing left to say. I awoke the next morning feeling lighter than I'd ever felt before. Divine intercession had arrived. I could laugh at my grim fate, and I no longer felt the need to conceal my shame because there was no more shame. I had been healed and could continue on the journey with a much lighter heart.

When we cannot break free from the tense concern over money there is but one thing to do: pray. We can only escape the emotional shackles of worry or concern over money fears when we seek the deep and profound silence within, for it is in the silence where purity emerges and washes us clean. We ask God to free us from all burdens, worries, and concerns. God will release us from all that has a vise-grip on our peace of mind. We can count on God. Always.

Prayer can save the day when we're in one helluvah negative stupor, and we can use the power of prayer to redesign our lives and get back on track when we cannot do it alone. Life hurts sometimes. Akin to a spiteful lover, our money concerns will find every button to push, leaving us too worn out and incapable of breaking free of the dark, vicious thought pattern that engulfs us. Our reprieve is prayer. It is the peaceful highway out of hell. It illuminates the soul and releases negativity from the mind. We can press on with the journey once we allow prayer to swathe us in comfort. Our unlimited potential lies within, impregnated by heavenly expectation, from which a much better life can emerge. We save ourselves by salvaging our mortal mind. When we fill our mind with love and peace, love and peace flow into us like air into a balloon.

Prayer provides the conduit to Divine Guidance, and we are never disappointed by the overgenerous gifts Divine Guidance bestows. We become so attached to how life should occur for us, but ours is such a limited view. Our guardian angels see the bigger picture. It is in prayer that our eyes and ears are open to the Divine Guidance that's been waiting to be tapped into. We find real peace in fully releasing the outcome of whatever our circumstance may be and surrendering all concerns into divine hands. There are no better hands to be in. Your willingness to surrender is what will save you, so be willing to surrender. *Release and detach.* Whatever it is that blocks you from seeing an immediate solution to a problem can be revealed through the silent power of prayer. It will seem as though the resolution materializes out of thin air.

When my busy life clusters into a whirling dervish and I'm barely hanging on, I close my eyes against the wickedness of overwhelm, I slow my breathing and begin my reverent conversation with God: *"I surrender to you all my striving, all my concern and worry. I release the outcome of this situation into your hands. Take from me what I can no longer bear. Please help me. Please direct my footsteps, direct my mind…"* I pray until serenity gently returns, and I relax into the trust of knowing that everything will work out perfectly for me.

There have been times in my life that I have felt so hindered and trapped, frantically trying to find a solution to a dark problem that has me stopped dead in my tracks. In my desperation, the only prayer I could mutter was, *"Oh God, please give me the guts to live through this day."* This is where I access tranquility, and in that state of tranquility I realize my faith once again. It is by grace that I no longer squander a day by hoping it will end swiftly because my emotions were spinning out of control.

Prayer was the lifeline that carried me through my darkest, most doubtful hours of emotional toxicity. I'd become so suppressed, unable to break free from the chains of self-doubt and self-loathing. Praying in the morning and each night hushed the voices in my weary head that detoured my inner harmony. When your mind races and you feel backed into a corner, only a spiritual connection can sober you. You are intended to ascend, and praying causes your frame of mind to shift instantly. When darkness looms from the unexpected bill that arrives, don't ignore it. Lift the concern over it into the light. Prayer strengthens your intuitive strengths and can unleash your miraculous powers of thought, emotion, and imagination that get stifled under a financial quagmire.

We've become spiritually starved; we crave a spiritual connection so badly we can taste it. God is in every circumstance, and when the mystifying occurs, it's God telling us he's here. When we invest in our faith, we graciously reinvest in ourselves. The moment we reach out to God, our lives are graced with enough light to receive prayer's generous compensation, and the psychic pain can dissipate.

Be mindful of God's many blessings. They are everywhere. Bless everything and everyone around you and notice how wildly alive you begin to feel. When fear looms the evening before a stressful appointment like a job interview, call to mind the people you'll encounter during the interview and bless them with your thoughts. See angels circling around the building where the interview will take place and imagine the building or office surrounded in beautiful white luminous light. Bless everyone and everything and notice that instantly you feel connected to something sacred and primal. Such peace will flood your mind, yielding the most beautiful outcome to that interview.

We may resist the ten minutes of praying, writing our affirmations, or deliberately using our imagination to create something better, but doing nothing different only keeps us stuck in mediocrity. It is when we are not deeply reflective that the shit hits the fan. Prayer is the only antidote to put us back into alignment with peace.

This is your opportunity to live life in a way that your ancestors would have thought to be that of legends. Yours is a truly magical life. Pay homage to your own connection and allow Spirit to move through you. Lift your gaze upward and beseech the heavens when a burning desire stirs your soul.

God loves us no matter what we did or didn't do, yet we think we need to be pretty saintly in order to knock on God's door. We do not. Knock. He'll answer. How are those knees of yours? Good. Strike a pose, as we say in unison, "Amen. "

I surrender all my concerns to God.

I see myself placing all my worries into the palm of God's hand.

God created me, and I can create anything I want with my magic wands.

> "You pray in your distress and in your need; would that you might also pray in the fullness of your joy and in your days of abundance."
> **-Khalil Gibran**

> "We can be tired, weary and emotionally distraught, but after spending time alone with God, we find that He injects into our bodies with energy, power and strength."
> **-Charles Stanley**

I now easily and effortlessly earn over $_____ each year.

TODAY'S GOALS
Surround yourself with those who contribute to the dream, and together you will thrive.

_____ _____
_____ _____
_____ _____
_____ _____
_____ _____

THINGS FOR WHICH I'M GRATEFUL
Once upon a time, there lived mesmerizing, captivating you.
Your life can have fairytale magic if you want it to.

_____ _____
_____ _____
_____ _____

AFFIRMATIONS
Feel big time joy as you fantasize money filling your closets, filling your drawers and making your wallet so full, it's bursting at the seams. Money comes to you from everywhere. Charging your vision with such epic emotions gives it epic creative power.

_____
_____
_____
_____
_____
_____
_____
_____
_____
_____

All you need is love.

Day 27 – Synchronicities: Cosmic Coincidences

"Keep your eyes open and your ears tuned for evidence of God's will working on your behalf. Especially in a moment of indecision, when someone unexpectedly or unknowingly pierces your consciousness with a bit of advice that rings true, recognize that God is speaking by proxy. If you are discerning, miracles can happen." -Albert Clayton Gaulden

It happens often enough. We think of someone we haven't seen or heard from in ages, and we soon bump into them or they call us on the phone. "I was just thinking about you," we tell them. What is that? Coincidence? Does my thinking of them strangely cause them to connect with me in some way, or does my mind get some advance indication of our meeting? Or you're merrily singing a song. You get in the car and turn on the radio. A sudden chill prickles your spine: that same song is now playing on the radio. No one is immune to it. At one time or another, we all experience it. But what does it mean? It's coincidence, we tell ourselves again. Or is it perhaps something more? Often times, we're too busy to pay attention, so we dismiss it.

Carl Jung called it "synchronicity": two seemingly unrelated events that cannot be explained by cause and effect, but are uniquely linked by personal meaning. Since we're a little freaked out by it, we comfortably choose to call it coincidence. Or luck. Chance. Fate. Happenstance. Serendipity. A fluke or a lucky break. We call it everything but what it really is: our cosmic support, the driving forces at work behind the scenes. Divine Guidance in perfect form. We're being soul-directed, and we get goose bumps every time.

We receive the money just in the nick of time. We meet the right person at the right moment that ends up steering us in the right direction. We pick up a book and read the very thing we need to know at that moment. We're one car ahead of a horrific car accident. We paint ourselves into a corner and have exhausted every avenue for a way out. There's nothing more we can do but wait for divine intervention. And then it shows up. The whole thing smacks of magic. The heavens are always involved in the affairs of humans, and synchronicities are evidence of it.

Synchronous circumstances demonstrate how we draw to us the experiences that dovetail perfectly with where we are in our inner life. They tend to appear more often during the times of significant personal transformation. They provide the sacred groundwork for our mission, but on the surface they seem to be illogical and irrational. I sense the endless churning in that mind of yours. Making sense, losing sense. Stop thinking so much and just be with the mystery.

Limitations only reside within the mortal mind. We become so fixated on what the perfect job will look like, or how we'll amp up our income. Our firm expectation of how or when our miracles will occur deafens our ears to the direction of the heavens. Such an ego-driven perspective distracts us from our inner guidance and throws us off far course. Exquisite epiphanies arise when we allow spirit to direct our every thought, word, and action. Only when we are centered within ourselves can the miracles unfold easily and effortlessly.

Everyday epiphanies bestow life's abundant blessings on us if we're open and receptive to receiving them. We do this be being attuned to our inner wisdom. Synchronicities communicate information to us in resourceful ways, yet we cannot hear them until we silence the inner noise. We have no idea how things will pan out for us, but they will. If we didn't get the job, we weren't meant to. Something better, something more extraordinary is on its way. Once we live from the vantage point that we are always at the right place at the right time, we surely will be. When we're attuned to our radar, we can encode the messages we are given and fit the pieces together. By casting our view to the heavens instead of the sidewalk for direction, we allow our footsteps to be divinely guided. Silence gives rise to the listening. Thou shalt silence the inner noise; otherwise you won't hear the direction being given. Praying for divine guidance and asking that our footsteps go where God would have them go *is* the way to go. It is with prayer, meditation and visualization that we gain access to our intuitive strengths. The perfect insights come to us after time spent in prayer or meditation that wouldn't have emerged if our minds were not allowed to quiet. Intentionality with our thoughts, emotions, and imaginings not only quiets the mind; it grants a meaningful and peaceful inner life. It is here where conditions are ripe for effortless manifestation.

Throughout the course of life, we wind up at crossroads brought on by some affliction like a job loss, a monetary collapse, or the ending of a relationship, and sometimes the direction to take is not clear. Our path is about to change and a daunting fear of the unknown scares the hell out of us. The internal voices are especially strong when we find ourselves at such a turning point. We know the voices by now. They clip our wings if we allow them any power. Yet the voices sound so dang convincing. *I don't know what to do. How am I going to make it? I'm such a fool. I don't make good choices. I'm going to fail and everyone will say they told me so. I'm so confused. I'd better ask everyone else what I should do because I can't trust even myself.* Then we look out the window like we'll get an answer from the sky or something. Ho-hum.

When our desire is so strong, and the timing is right for the next evolution of our soul, signals for support are sent out to the four corners of the Universe, and the perfect assistance is drawn to us. When our head is noisy and big, and there's no visible light at the end of our dark tunnel vision, providence intervenes. We glimpse the light at the end of the tunnel once we feel the ethereal forces holding our hand as we walk through it. Cloaked in sacred and primal mystery, these cosmic messengers are always at work behind the scenes. Once we allow them to steer us in the direction of abundance, abundance will be delivered. Each of us have guardian angels assigned to us at birth, and they remain with us throughout our lifetime. Their ethereal assignment is to guide us towards whatever will bring us joy. Without them, we're lost souls. They're waiting for us to wake up and start living the dream. They deliver fate to our doorstep and cheer us on as we take flight towards our dreams. They provide us ascension above the voices, so fear has less sway over our internal state. They're always in attendance, providing us communion with who we really are, restoring our pure connection to God. We've simply been unaware of their presence.

These invisible forces are always guiding us to a rich life of mystery, intrigue, and beauty. They're waiting in the wings (no pun intended), and they want to help. At any time, at any place, we can call upon our cosmic support system. Whatever is missing can surely be found once we ask for divine guidance. In the midst of emotional turmoil and unrest, we can access these divine messengers once we quiet the mind. Our cosmic support system never fails to lift our hearts high above the din and strife, allowing us to regain the perspective to see the bigger picture. Yet we must manage our negative emotions in order to hear the direction they are so eager to provide.

We block divine guidance with our anger, fear, and frustration, so venturing into the silence in which all things begin is quintessential. We seek sustenance from our spiritual hunger and refuge from the external world in prayer and meditation. It is here where we tap into the divinity within that allows inner peace once again.

Divine forces can save the day even before it's started. Angels go to work on us as we sleep and rearrange our energies, washing away all negativity from the day, restoring to us our creative power so we are able to press on. Our needs are always taken care of, as long as we're willing to follow the inner guidance that leads us safely to whatever it is we seek-shelter, food, happiness, the new job, the bigger income. Our cosmic partners want to be given tasks, and they are never too distant to hear our requests. We cannot sit around waiting for the miracles to arrive either. This will only stall the process. Instead, we carry on with life, allowing love and joy to flow generously from our heart as we remain open to receiving the divine direction in whatever form it takes. We're all guided. If you want to learn how to generate prosperity, you'll be led to a teacher who can help you. All requests are heard, and all requests are granted. All we need to do is ask and invoke the powers of love and joy to clear the pathway to their guidance. They will attract to us the perfect people, books, classes, and situations that further the expedition to our magnificent kismet. They even led you to this book. It may not occur immediately or in the way we think it should occur, but it will always occur if it is requested.

There are no accidents. Everything is by design, and that's the point. Divine forces can make our journey an easier path to tread if we're open to hearing their directives. The directives of our soul speak to us through our intuition. The quiet voice you hear from time to time urging you towards something that feels right- these are the guiding voices of angels. The angels often speak directly to our hearts as we sleep, so pay attention to your dreams. You can open a book and whatever you need to know is right there. If the thought of someone or a certain place or event continues to enter your mind, contact that person or go to the place or event that keeps popping up in your head. Anytime you see or hear something repeatedly, take heed. It may mean that you're on the cusp of something grand occurring for you.

We are never alone. The angels use the energy of synchronicities to support us in our quest, and they're waiting to be called upon at any given moment. Synchronous happenings are evidence of angels gathering around us and drawing to us that which we are requesting. It feels like fairy dust has been sprinkled on us every time it occurs. We may have a sudden revelation or a physical reaction in our gut. Intuitive messages may begin to break through, nudging us toward something that gets us closer to prosperity. Or we may find that we're at the right place at the right time.

We feel the presence of our ethereal friends when there is an overwhelming feeling of warmth and love, a sense of security and reassurance, or a tingling sensation in our arms or legs. Receiving kindness from others may be the calling card of an angel, so never refuse kindness from others.

Your winged guardians are waiting to assist you in the quest for abundance. You are being divinely guided in every moment with infinite wisdom and deep love. Synchronicities spur you on in the direction you need to go. The signs are all around you. They communicate to you in very inventive ways, so look for the clues, the keys to unlock the doors. Be receptive and alert-on a constant lookout for the synchronicities that will now occur for you. Believe me; they will occur with great frequency the more you align yourself with your angelic powers. If someone suggests something new for you to try, try it. If a book sounds interesting to you, read it. Pay close attention to your dreams. Follow your hunches. Live on the assumption that there are no accidents. Allow yourself to wonder, *"Where will I be led today?"* You'll easily be swept toward a life of prosperity by a benevolent flow of synchronicities.

Salute the angels the next time you receive a divine hint or have a divine encounter. You experience the glory of your creation when little things begin to occur that are unexplainable. It's a tip off that you're onto to something, so keep going. The more open-minded you are and the bigger you dare to dream, the greater your opportunities and possibilities. With faith, synchronicities become a way of life-a divinely directed way of life.

Angels are rallying around you. They've never left your side. Can you feel them? Allow them to gently guide you along your personal journey and coax you towards your destiny. Know that you're divinely guided, always. Everything arrives at its appointed hour. You simply need to trust that you will be ushered on to greatness. Be so attuned to the forces of divine guidance that you feel the tip of an angel's wing brush your arm.

I am continually met with spellbinding coincidences.

My life is one of adventure. Every day is a new beginning. I wonder what will happen next?

> "Believers, look up - take courage. The angels are nearer than you think."
> **-Billy Graham**

> "My own life has been touched often by synchronicity, so much so that now I get on an airplane expecting the passenger in the next seat to be surprisingly important to me, either just the voice I need to hear to solve a problem or a missing link in a transaction that needs to come together...I believe that all coincidences are messages from the unmanifest – they are like angels without wings, so to speak, sudden interruptions of life by a deeper level."
> **-Deepak Chopra**

> "The dreams which reveal the supernatural are promises and messages that God sends us directly: they are nothing but His angels, His ministering spirits, who usually appear to us when we are in a great predicament. "
> **-Paracelsus**

I now easily and effortlessly earn over $_____each year.

Angels work for God. They are masters of love. If you only knew who walked beside you, never again would you be lonely, worried, or afraid.

TODAY'S GOALS

Seek the wisdom of your soul. Be receptive and allow Divine forces to guide you today. If you feel you should go to a certain place, go. If someone recommends a book to you, read it. Is there a certain movie that is calling to you? Be open to it all.

_____   _____

_____   _____

_____   _____

_____   _____

THINGS FOR WHICH I'M GRATEFUL

Apply the power of love in every conversation, ever thought, every action.

_____   _____

_____   _____

_____   _____

AFFIRMATIONS

You have money coming to you from everywhere. See it. Feel it. Believe it. *And you will have it.*

_____

_____

_____

_____

_____

_____

_____

_____

_____

_____

Day 28 – Paying Bills

"If you don't want to be there--don't go there!" -Sallye Taylor

For many of us, bill paying can be hell. When we're up to our eyeballs in bills, the more out of whack our emotions are and the further we sink into financial torment. And why is this? Hold yourself, dear. Because our magic wand of emotion is being fueled by anger and fear, and it casts a magic spell out to the universe that returns to us the physical representation of those emotions: more and more bills. Ahhhhhk!

Since bill paying can be an activity of angst, we'll want to employ a new strategy to trick the mind into believing we actually enjoy the experience. That's right. We'll learn to love the mailbox and our mail! This lends a hand in creating the new brain pattern that brings us abundance instead of more bills, and we prefer the latter much, much more. We've conditioned ourselves to believe that paying bills is a stressful event, even downright torturous. When I was a youngster, we knew it was not a good idea to bother my dad when he was paying bills, but one night I needed help with my homework. There he was. Sitting at the dining room table, pen in hand, burning cigarette in the other, checkbook open, and a pile of bills so high they looked like he was building a paper fort on top of the table. "Dad, I need help with my math," I said. He looked at me like he was possessed by Lucifer and screamed, "Get the hellllll outtttta here! Damn it! Can't you see I'm under the gun!!" He puffed so hard on that cigarette you would have thought it was his turn to be executed in front of a firing squad. I knew bills must be bad. They must be really, really bad if they could make my dad look that terrified. When he said he was 'under the gun', you would have thought a Smith and Wesson was pointed right in his direction.

We are far too fabulous to risk the dangerous financial manifestation of a declining mood, so we're going to shift the energy of the bill paying experience. Here's how: Buy yourself a pretty pen that you'll use only for bill paying, and find a file folder with a nice pattern on the outside to hold your bills and keep them organized. Set aside a half hour each week to quietly and consciously organize your bills and settle the accounts you owe. Clear your desk or table from clutter. Light a candle. Put on some mood music. Now get comfortable and take some slow, deep breaths from your abdomen. Begin to organize and pay those bills with lots of love and lots of joy. As you look at your electric or gas bill, feel immense gratitude for having enough money to pay that bill. In your mind, say thank you to the gas or electric company for trusting you enough to settle the bill after you've already used the service. Write out the check, give it a little kiss for good luck, and know, without a doubt, that more money is coming your way. Place it lovingly in the envelope, put a stamp on it, and move along to the next bill. Thank each company that sent you their bill, feel lots of gratitude, and kiss each check for good luck.

Since everything is made up of energy, you can pay for these services more serenely, even when you're financially strapped, by remembering that all financial transactions are simply an exchange of energy. Someone provides us services in the form of heat, light, food, gas, clothing, medical care, or shelter, and we pay for these services with energy in the form of money. If you pay your bills electronically through online banking, the energy is simply shuffled from one account to another.

There is an unlimited amount of energy in the Universe, and we can tap into that supply if we don't block the Universe's stream of good with our own negative emotions. We can keep a constant flow of money in our daily lives through giving with love and paying what we owe with gratitude.

Not settling the debts we owe in a timely manner can turn our world upside down quickly, and there's a vicious snowball effect that ensues. If we're not paying our bills on time, there's an emotional and a financial impact we experience, and it isn't pretty. How much time and emotional energy do we squander making excuses to bill collectors or to those we owe money? Bill collectors trespass all over our peace of mind, and we wind up wanting to cry our brains out.

We further add to our financial difficulty if we are delinquent in paying a utility bill. The service gets shut off, plus an extra fee to have it turned back on. Any sense of sanity is destroyed when the utility company arrives at our home to turn the service on again. It is here that we're subjected to the misgivings of shame, panic, and anger that'll give us diarrhea for days. *"What will the neighbors think?"* the voices ask, like we're the laughing stock of our own church now. We want to escape two thousand miles away and take our shameful shame with us. Our inner worlds create our outer reality. This is universal law. It's not simply the hefty fee we must pay to have the utility turned back on; there's an even heftier fee we pay once peace of mind has gone missing.

Sometimes we don't pay certain bills at all. Move forward a scene. Stop! Instead of getting into communication and arranging to settle the bill in monthly installments, or working a part-time job until the debt is cleared, we invest enormous amounts of time and negative energy into writing letters filled with excuses to our debtors. This type of investment never pays well. The energy we extend out into the universe will always return to us. It always does.

We suffer a panic attack when the mail arrives, and we may even wait days to retrieve the contents from the mailbox to delay the reality that waits. We create so much emotional angst and drama around the mailbox experience that when we finally summon the courage to retrieve our mail, our walk to the mailbox becomes more like a walk to the electric chair. No wonder we drown in debt. No wonder our utilities get shut off.

There, there, my quivering dew drop. It's alright. I assure you that you are dealing with a brain pattern that causes you such distress. The mailbox experience only serves as a mirror of your inner dialogue. You can trick the mind into believing something new, so you attract checks in the mail instead of bills. Shall I give you an example?

Consider revamping your mail box, so it's inviting. Paint it so it's pretty. That's right. Make it pretty, so you change the energy field around it. You can even paint it so it looks like it's covered in money. Plant some pretty flowers around it. Begin affirming that money arrives in the mail from expected and unexpected resources. And when the mail arrives, put some energetic music on your iPod and stick some ear buds in to distract your mind from the negative programming that has you believing you'll be electrocuted when you open the mailbox door. Do whatever works for you to create a new brain pattern that graciously welcomes the mail, and the USPS will deliver prosperity to you.

You can knock off days in purgatory left and right just by doing the work here. To create a new brain pattern that brings you abundance in the mail, repeat your affirmations, mind your emotions, and use that imagination of yours to create splendor in paradise. You're creating every single corner of your world to be prosperous. This is one corner that may need a little sprucing up. Make the brilliant decision to put some full-blown integrity into your bill paying approach. You're a superior manifestor, so act like one. Honor your debts and do so with love and joy, and what returns to you will be Ahhmaazing!

You are pure love, and so many untapped gifts of yours are soon to be discovered. The universe is at your command. Continue on with repeating your two affirmations. Repeat them hundreds of times each day. Write them as often as you can. Sing them. Dance while you sing them. Visualize an unlimited bank account for yourself. See yourself paying your bills with ease and grace, feeling joyful and happy all the while through. Then all there is to do is sit back and allow all the goodness to come easily into your life. You're going to make a lot of money. *I mean a lot of money.*

The more responsible I become, the farther my wings reach.

I think of the things I want, and I see them as already manifested in my life.

Abundance always surrounds me. Today I claim my share.

> "The walls we build around us to keep sadness out also keeps out the joy."
> **-Jim Rohn**

> "What we think determines what happens to us, so if we want to change our lives, we need to stretch our minds."
> **- Wayne Dyer**

I now easily and effortlessly earn over $_____ each year.

Who wouldn't want my life?! It's amazing!

TODAY'S GOALS
You're creating a life you love, and goals are where the creation of it begins, you little genius, you.

_____   _____
_____   _____
_____   _____
_____   _____

THINGS FOR WHICH I'M GRATEFUL
All the goodness that exists in the world yearns to find you. Allow it to easily find its way.

_____   _____
_____   _____
_____   _____

AFFIRMATIONS
You always win, and no one else must lose in order for you to win.

_____
_____
_____
_____
_____
_____
_____
_____

Set a timer at every hour on the hour as a reminder to do brief 20-30 second visualization exercises throughout the day. Use your emotions to charge your visualizations and fully concentrate your mind on your visions.

Day 29 - Who We Are and Who We Can Become

"The deepest secret is that life is not a process of discovery, but a process of creation. You are not discovering yourself, but creating yourself anew. Seek therefore, not to find out who you are, but seek to determine who you want to be." –Neale Donald Walsch

Let's be honest. We really don't want to take responsibility for ourselves, our lives, or our circumstances. We have such firmly held beliefs like, "*That's what God has given me,*" or "*This is my lot in life.*" By thinking such thoughts, we establish resolutely set boundaries that make it incredibly difficult to break through. Remember, our emotional reality is always our own responsibility-no one else's-yet we continue to play the blame game. We give away our power by blaming the circumstance, blaming others, blaming the economy, and emotionally reacting to the situation, instead of choosing to respond to the situation with an emotion of our own choosing. The obstruction to our greatness is always the result.

Hell is knowing who you really are and not being that. A larger life is latent in human beings, and it's begging to be revealed. The soul knows all there is to know. It's been calling to us all along. The soul is experiential; it wants to feel and experience as much as it can. You were created to experience the magnificence of who you really are and who you can be. We are spirits living in a human body, and our quest lies in breaking through our humanity, the machine, to call forth the divine magnificence of which we really are. The more you live in alignment with who you really are at the level of the soul (loving, joyous, and gracious), the more you can become. The more you become, the more you can be.

Who we are as human beings is a culmination of different ways of *being*. We can be loving, confident, abundant, bold, cheerful, powerful, fun, happy, optimistic, joyful, responsible, and courageous. Conversely, we can also be meek, negative, impoverished, broke, sad, depressed, angry, timid, cynical, afraid, and irresponsible. These are all ways of being. Our ways of being are the result of our attitude, our state of mind, our emotional state, our bodily state, our thoughts, and our thought processes. Our existing ways of being have simply been the expressions of the dominant brain patterns we've had in place for years. These brain patterns ultimately create who we're being at any given time, unless we deliberately choose to be something different.

Our primary purpose is to create. It is why we have been gifted with such vastly creative powers to begin with. Some ways of being work well for us and cause effectiveness in certain areas of life; other ways of being cause ineffectiveness in other areas. Our energy is projected out into the world for physical manifestation through our thoughts, our emotions, our conversations, and our imaginings. It is in *who we are being* that determines the ingredients in the creative energy that we emit. Let's take a look at our ways of being with our money, shall we?

Consider that who we are being in our finances is negative, fearful, and doubtful. If that's how we're being, what emotions are we having? Our emotions are most likely negative, insecure, depressed, fearful, and anxious. What bodily responses do we have to these emotions? We may have an upset stomach, nervousness, uneasiness, and tension in the neck and shoulders. What are the thoughts we're thinking when we're being this way? *I can't afford that. I never have enough money. Life sucks. I'm tired. I can't do it. This is too hard. I hate bills. I don't make enough money. I'm such a failure. I'm scared.* The actions we take are always consistent with our way of being. What actions do we take when we're being negative, irresponsible, and fearful? We complain a great deal. We make poor choices, and we mismanage our money. We stay at a job that doesn't pay us very well. Sometimes we take no action at all, which is part of the problem. The brain pattern is apparent. This negative transmission of energy is emitted through our negative way of being with money, and we no choose to be this way any longer.

Knowing something and experiencing something are two completely different things. We know that prosperity will bring us joy. The purpose of the soul is to turn the knowing of prosperity into the experience of joy and peace of mind that is brought forth by being prosperous. It is in *being* joyful that we attract all that represents joy for us, prosperity included. This is the order of it all: knowing, experiencing, then being. If we change our way of being, we change our circumstances. And so, boys and girls, we change from the inside out. All too often, we focus on the problem at hand instead of looking for the way of being that created the problem in the first place. As long as we continually explore the problem, we remain stuck with the problem. It does not matter who you are right now, but who you want to be. You are here to experience glory to the max. You are a pure creative spirit, and all circumstances offer you the opportunity to choose to be who you really are. Instead of condemning your financial circumstances, bring forth a way of being that you'd like to experience in the midst of that circumstance.

To be or not to be. That is the choice. Sure, you'd like to have a brain switch with Donald Trump or Heidi Klum. Guess what? You can! Sort of. Act like your heroes. Read about them. Watch them. Listen to them. Emulate a new way of being based on those you admire most and practice that intentionally for five days in a row. This new way of being will become a dominant one that will begin to arise naturally. During my personal transformation, I had lots of pictures of Jackie Kennedy Onassis on my Vision Board. I admired her beauty, her elegance, her gracefulness, and her style. She reeked of class, and I wanted to be just like her. Years later, I'm often told by others that I remind them of Jackie O. I find it wonderfully amusing. I emanate her ways of being because I practiced them. I imagined me being just like her. What I know now is that my life is a pure self-creation. Yours can be, too.

"I am" is a powerful creative statement. *"I am abundant in all areas of life,"* creates the experiences of that. How do we create a new way of being amid the painful jolting of constant financial scarcity? By slowing down. By concentrating on one breathe at a time. By stating, *"I am peace of mind"* and allowing peace of mind to arise as if it were the only thing worth doing at the moment.

Yet, there are times when possibility goes missing, and we're left feeling uninspired about life. We access our inner power when we become the highest vision of ourselves. To make a radical shift in your internal state, try the exercise below:

Action: Envisioning Your New Life

Get comfortable and allow your mind to quiet. Call to mind the very highest thought you could possibly have of yourself. Your thought might be *"I am wildly successful in all areas of life."* Imagine the 'you' that you would be if you lived that thought every day. What thoughts would you think? What would you do and say? How would you respond to what others do and say? Allow yourself to clearly imagine who you'd be, living this magnificent vision of yourself. Stay in your imagination for about a minute and focus on the details of your image. Once you open your eyes, begin to intentionally create your thoughts, emotions, words, and actions to match the vision you had in your imagination. Now go about your day and amaze yourself.

We are never stuck living a life we don't love. We're never stuck being a certain way. No, no, no. Our minds are like star gates. Think different. Feel different. Be different. You're on the cusp of a personal evolution. You're free as a bird and can generate unlimited ways of being, and you can do so on command. Since our ways of being are self-created, you can choose to be any way you want.

You're more dazzling than a glitter pop, and you're living at full blast with the volume cranked way up. Generate from within and extend it outward. How wonderful you don't need to wait one more moment for the tide to change. It is a birth of a new you. Be not who you were 'supposed' to be, but who you choose to be. The next time you're in a bad situation and you don't know what to do, act like one of your heroes. Or try being a Top Gun, a Black Belt, or an Army Ranger. You are the Lauren Bacall of your hometown and don't you forget it. You'll notice that people are suddenly drawn to your stunning personality. Today, tell yourself that you can do and be absolutely anything you choose. Because, my dear friend, you can.

I am always happy no matter what.

I practice feeling happy on a daily basis and abundance is always the result.

> "To be a great champion, you must believe you are the best. If you're not, pretend you are."
> **-Mohammad Ali**

> "Who am I then? Tell me that first, and then, if I like being that person, I'll come up; if not, I'll stay down here till I'm someone else."
> **— Lewis Carroll**
> *Alice's Adventures in Wonderland & Through the Looking-Glass*

I now easily and effortlessly earn over $_____**each year.**

Feelings of profound joy and happiness are constant for me.

TODAY'S GOALS

Five minutes a day is all that is required. Use your emotions to charge your visualizations, and concentrate your mind. Then list your goals and be a high-caliber performing engine today!

_____ _____

_____ _____

_____ _____

_____ _____

THINGS FOR WHICH I'M GRATEFUL

What is it you dream of?

_____ _____

_____ _____

_____ _____

AFFIRMATIONS

Your mind is always listening.

_____

_____

_____

_____

_____

_____

_____

_____

_____

_____

You are destined for greatness. You know this, right?

Day 30 - Navy SEALS

"The ability to control my emotions and my actions, regardless of circumstance, sets me apart from other men. Uncompromising integrity is my standard. My character and honor are steadfast. My word is my bond...I will never quit. I persevere and thrive on adversity. My Nation expects me to be physically harder and mentally stronger than my enemies. If knocked down, I will get back up, every time. I am never out of the fight...I will not fail."
–from the U.S. Navy SEAL's Creed

They operate at sea, in the air, and on land. U.S. Navy SEALS are a Special Forces group so elite they don't accept applications. Members are silently recruited. SEALs put their lives on the line defending our country against some of the most diabolical minds that exist, and each member of that team knows, without one single shadow of a doubt, that the man fighting alongside of him will never give in or punk out when the situation gets hellish. These top secret elite warriors are the best of their kind in the entire world. They're hard core and get the job done that no one else can. Armed to the teeth, these shadow warriors move stealthily through the darkness. They can survive arctic conditions and can endure exposure to tear gas. They jump from planes eleven miles up in the air, sit for prolonged periods of time in deadly silence, camouflage themselves in any environment, and hold their breath underwater for more than two minutes without releasing a single bubble. They break down enemy doors and shoot with deadly, pinpoint precision. The deadliest weapon a SEAL has is his unwavering mental discipline that makes him shockingly capable of withstanding the most unthinkable physical constraints.

Known for an intense training regimen that takes up to two years to complete, it's not difficult to understand why only 75 percent of the candidates make it through. Fear and self-doubt are trained right out of them during the torturous final days of SEAL training. Welcome to Hell Week-the ultimate determination of who has the guts, the physical ability, and the pure mental toughness to endure. For 132 hours straight, candidates push their bodies and their minds to the limits. Sleep deprived and kept in constant motion, they are plunged 350 feet underwater with their hands and feet bound. If panic dare set in, they're done. Every minute is a race, and recruits are kept constantly cold and constantly wet. Trainees carry heavy boats overhead everywhere they go, and much of that final week is spent swimming against the unforgiving heavy waves of frigid, icy sea water. Teeth chatter as hypothermia begins to set in, and wet sand burns their weary eyes and chafes at their raw skin, yet the pain they endure when their bodies are screaming to quit pales in comparison to the pain of quitting. A burning desire to succeed is what allows a SEAL to persevere despite unfathomable physical exhaustion and sleep deprivation.

It's the primal burn of destiny calling that drives them to keep their eyes on the target and train with a purpose. This is how mental discipline is acutely developed. You concentrate on the end goal and train your mind daily as if your life depends on it. Because it does.

Having such an intense desire to succeed and prosper in life is what will fuel the fire in your belly to such a fevered pitch that you'd rather die than quit with your mental discipline. You're no different than a Navy SEAL. Your mind training is voluntary. You can stop at any time, but it's up to you to build an internal inferno strong enough to keep you motivated to develop your mental discipline. The agony of failure must be greater than your resistance to doing the daily mind work; otherwise you're destined to be defeated by your daily financial circumstances. Having a burning desire to succeed with your mental discipline doesn't just happen. Every action you take is the result of a decision you've chosen. The intensity of your desire is correlated to the number of decisions you make to get you to your goal. You're either committed or you're not. There is no grey here. You either go for it with everything you've got or don't bother trying. The decision is yours. Right now ask yourself: "How badly do I want it, and what am I willing to sacrifice to get it?"

Ask any SEAL and he'll tell you the most vicious battlefield that exists is the one in the mind. The mental strength of a SEAL will *always* dominate on *any* battlefield. We're at war right now, and the enemy we face on the battlefield is a troop of unrelenting demons. The sniper: those defeatist voices in our head that take no prisoners. Appropriate measures must be taken to silence the enemy. Our own private apocalypse impales us when we come under withering enemy fire; things start unraveling quickly once the adversary strikes Fear in us. Our negative head chatter- the pessimistic money beliefs we inked on paper earlier in this course-is the enemy. The atmosphere in our head is never good during such an invasion. The enemy voices kick in when we let our guard down. They tell us we must work hard to get anywhere in this world. They tell us we'll never succeed; we don't have what it takes to thrive. The voices tell us to give up on our dreams; to quit hoping things will actually turn out for us. The casualty count rises once the mind begins to believe in its fragility. We want to give up and retreat by playing small again when we're stormed and besieged by a nasty negative funk brought on by enemy forces.

Armed with a new kind of defense, our mental toughness begins the depleting enemy resources. If we get slammed by the bills that arrive in the mail, the negative voices will be with us for most of that day, giving us all sorts of reasons why we shouldn't continue on with our mental discipline. Their intention is to stop us. Their goal is to cause emotional suffering. Just know this: these incessant, self-deflating voices will eventually grow quieter, but they will never really go away. When their entrenched air strike begins, the only effective strategy to disarm them is to ignore them, for this is the ground strategy for overcoming them. The voices will provide us with excuses to quit, all of which we will IGNORE, IGNORE, IGNORE.

We're fighting an all out ground war, jungle war, and aerial war when we're besieged by the emotional exclamation marks that come from the suffering of being financially broken. When we're physically exhausted and breaking down emotionally and mentally, we develop ourselves further by ignoring the voices when they cross the border of our mind and raid our joy and peace.

When physical, emotional and mental exhaustion set in, the voices are free to take control, and unconventional warfare is necessary for the counterattack on such hostile forces. When it gets so tense, we just know the marines are coming; it's our commitment and determination that will see us through. Mental discipline can be developed. We accomplish this when we train with a purpose. We want to work on ourselves for five minutes a month, but mental discipline and strength takes consistent practice. Just *thinking* about doing the work isn't the same thing as doing it. If we have time to watch TV, complain, space out, or chat on the phone for longer than five minutes, we have the necessary time to adopt a new mental mindset. From this day forward, all non-essential activities are being curtailed. We're on a reconnaissance mission to begin the invasion of enemy lines. Training begins today, soldier.

We have within us the seeds for achieving our goals, but we sure can run at the mouth when we wake up agitated as hell. Whatever our dreams are, we'll turn them into our worst nightmares if we don't feed them positivity. No big deal. We've got things under control. No matter how exhausted you may be, and no matter how badly you feel after yet another financial collapse, you will NEVER formalize these feelings by verbalizing them and giving them power. Instead, you'll say the opposite, *"Man, I feel good,"* or *"What a great day to be alive!"* The mere suggestion of such positive declarations plants powerful seeds in the mind. When you empty the entire negative contents of your brainpan on anyone who will listen, however, a very powerful suggestion is also planted in the mind that will grow into something you surely don't want to experience-another financial meltdown. Keep the nasty commentary to yourself and work through it until it dissipates. You'll get so positive on everyone in your house that they won't know what to do with you. It's your alleged good attitude that will always keep you in the money game.

Your mental discipline is further developed by being very detailed about the way you prepare for each new day. It's a firm lifestyle commitment that brings a new dimension to your routine, and it looks like this: set the alarm clock across the room, so you're not tempted to push the snooze button. When the alarm sounds, jump outta bed like a happy, go-lucky, bouncy spring! This gets the blood flowing immediately. You're in training to silence the inner voices urging you to give up on your efforts. Each morning, without fail, the deliberate practice of your money affirmations begins. Intentionally cause yourself to feel optimistic and enthusiastic about the miracles that await you each day. Only your thoughts about yourself prevent you from reaching any goal. Map out your daily goals that provide a continued sense of accomplishment, and rip through 15-20 more money affirmations before lunch, dinner, and bedtime. Got it?

To counter the attack of a roving band of voices that begin to enter the mind, quit feeling sorry for yourself and start again by employing the skill of visualization. If there's anything you want changed in your life, first imagine it changed. See yourself succeeding. *Always.* Now get in there and make magic happen in that imagination of yours.

You will never give up! When you train with an intended purpose, when you're committed and determined, then it's not a matter of how, but rather how soon you step into your divine capacity. Mental discipline is an evolution. Your training regimen is now in full force. This work is the access to financial bliss. You don't miss a day of employing the strategic efforts to gain access to that bliss. If you're about to cave in, imagine the enemy *not* caving in. You are a born leader, so take charge, or the machine will take the reins, and that's a war you most certainly don't want to engage in.

You can do this. Go long, stay strong and always ignore the voices. Be proud as hell of the work you've done here, soldier. You are one tough mudder and have earned the rank of Creative Master, First Class.

I am a disciplined prosperity master. I train for mental toughness each and every day. Because I do so, I can influence matter. I can alter my future. Therefore, I am in charge of my destiny.

I now easily and effortlessly earn over $_____each year.

Be the last one to ask how much something costs.

TODAY'S GOALS
"Energy and persistence conquer all things."
-Benjamin Franklin

THINGS FOR WHICH I'M GRATEFUL
You are generating energy constantly.
Be mindful of this and intentionally charge your energy with positivity.

AFFIRMATIONS
In order for you to manifest anything, you must nurture and grow the seed. Affirmations are focused thoughts. They are the seeds. Tend to your garden daily. Trust me. This stuff works.

Day 31 - Practice Makes Perfect.

"Do or do not. There is no try." -Yoda

Success isn't granted to a preordained few. That's not how it works. Success is available to us all. Abundance is universal and omnipresent, and there is more than enough to go around. Once we set our sights on our good fortune, there's no stopping us. But the key to staying in the money game is mastering our mental power.

Maybe you're familiar with the story of a young Michael Jordan who was cut from his high school basketball team during tryouts. Jordan didn't let the rejection stop him. Far from it. It fueled him to cultivate fierce unbreakable practice habits and a rigorous conditioning regimen that molded him into being one of the greatest athletes of all time. Talent had little to do with Jordan's success. Unwavering mental discipline was what propelled him into the same club as any of the other great achievers in the world.

Like any athlete who is a champion, we realize the importance of training and conditioning the muscles used to attain our every goal. We use the power of our thoughts to mold our reality. As the gap between our thoughts and our experienced reality becomes shorter and shorter, we resist time spent writing affirmations, praying, and deliberately imagining all the goodness we crave. We're unwilling to take the necessary time for such tedious tasks. We cannot merely dabble in this endeavor, or the results will be insignificant and sporadic. We'll stagnate in monetary mediocrity. If you want to settle for an average income, there's no need to bother with a routine involving the skills outlined in this manual. Either give everything you've got to this work or there's really no sense in trying. You were born for greatness, but you'll only achieve greatness through deliberate and consistent daily practice. It is the absolute source of great performance.

Elite performers practice deliberately and consistently every day, including weekends. From CEO's and professional athletes to the best musicians of all time and five-star chefs, those who perform at the top in their field devote endless hours in deliberate practice. For those of us who fear change, a new regimen can send us spinning into oblivion where the gods of the discombobulated are easily riled. All of our actions produce a like reaction. By creating a routine and adhering to it, we midwife all our dreams into fruition. A routine is a detailed course of action, a set of structures, to be followed at the same times each day. There is no substitute for the time spent in deliberate practice when a routine is followed. Ergo, heed my advice and put a sufficient regimen in place.

There is great power generated within our mind. A power so epic, we are capable of creating heaven or creating hell. Once you lay the mental plans of a routine, the liberation from financial peril occurs. How do your days typically begin? If the alarm goes off, and you hit the ground running like a bat out of hell to get your already-stressed-out-self out the door, feelings of fatigue, irritation, and overwhelm will gnaw at your nerves throughout the day. It's no wonder you're time-worn, senseless, and crazed half the time. Negative emotions diminish your brilliant potential. But you need not allow the negatives to hijack your morning. It's time you're carried off the battlefield of belief that you must struggle to prosper. In order to know a semblance of peace during the days of your life, a relaxed, well-planned morning allows the floodgates of goodness to fly wide open. Catch my drift?

Our minds are most receptive to receiving new ideas at the beginning of the day. The way in which we begin our day has a profound impact on the way the rest of the day will pan out. How we create our day, celebrate it, and consecrate it is exactly how we experience it. Take this on. It will be a real game changer for you. By beginning the day in a focused and centered fashion, we position ourselves to magnetize goodness in our direction. Out of nowhere astonishing gifts will appear.

Consistently practicing mental discipline was crucial for me to create a new money belief system that eventually produced the new brain pattern causing my breakthrough in abundance. I didn't know it at the time, but during my prosperity saga, my morning routine is what elevated me to a whole new realm of mental discipline. I'd wake up 30 minutes earlier than what I was accustomed to and consciously created my day the way I wanted it to unfold. The minute my feet hit the ground, I would declare out loud, *"I am a being of light, daughter of God. This day, only that which is for my highest good shall come to me."* Then out the door I'd go for a 20 minute walk with my dog, Opie, and I'd repeat two of my affirmations. One affirmation was repeated in my mind for the first 10 minutes of the walk, the second affirmation for another 10 minutes. Afterward, I'd sit in a comfortable chair and list my goals for the day. I'd read for a few minutes from one of my books on mind consciousness and say my daily prayers asking God for guidance. Another few minutes were spent expressing gratitude for all of the greatness that was appearing in my life. Then it was time to hit the shower, which was also part of my training ground. As I slathered my body with soap, I imagined I was also cleansing my mind of all negativity, and I'd chirp another round of affirmations.

Evidence of prosperity began to appear that further fueled my routine. Others began taking notice of just how lucky I was. After all, being lucky suggests that good things occur with complete ease and little effort. I decided I was lucky in all facets of life. As a result, luck consistently and magically found its way to me. It still does. I get the best parking spots. People offer me things for free on a regular basis. I get checks unexpectedly in the mail. Yada, yada, yada. Back then, ambition and self-improvement quickly became my fast new fate. I began looking forward to my morning routine because the impact of it was so powerful.

If you want to experience an ordinary, run of the mill, non-miraculous day, listen to the morning news. You're under construction, so steer clear of the news. You don't want any negativity interfering with your mind work. The easiest way to climb above the roar and eliminate chaos from your morning routine is to get up earlier. Combining some type of physical exercise with mental exercise is a bonus. Consciously designing your day impacts your quantum field.

Implement a sacred morning ritual that begins the minute you step foot out of bed and deliberately create every corner of your world. Light a candle and spend some time with God in the silence where the inner symphonies can be heard. Close your eyes and see yourself at a beautiful alter in nature. Allow warm, beautiful, spiritual light to flow through you. Visualize love radiating from within, and allow it to cleanse all of your fear-based thoughts and feelings. Ask for Divine Guidance to lead you throughout the day. Bless everything and everyone-even the people you don't like. Before you go to sleep tonight, tell yourself you'll sleep soundly, and awaken refreshed and energized. You were intended to live a big life, so begin your day big tomorrow.

We're wired to struggle, and only you can order a rewire and end the struggle with money once and for all. You must upgrade your system daily. The kitten won't purr before you pet it, and you are no longer casual about your prosperity training. You can hear the whispering of your soul if you listen close enough. Angels are applauding your progress. There's real magic in the early morning hours. Take advantage of it.

I now easily and effortlessly earn over $_____each year.

TODAY'S GOALS

Don't know the answer to the question? Can't find a solution to the problem? Go within and quiet your mind. The perfect answer or solution will arise at the perfect time.

_____ _____

_____ _____

_____ _____

_____ _____

THINGS FOR WHICH I'M GRATEFUL

Give a wink and a nod to your guardian angels every time something good happens for you.

_____ _____

_____ _____

_____ _____

AFFIRMATIONS

I always have more than enough money to pay my bills with ease.

Day 32 - An Attitude of Gratitude

"Gratitude bestows reverence, allowing us to encounter everyday epiphanies, those transcendent moments of awe that change forever how we experience life and the world." -John Milton

The sunset is taking its time today, and that's a-ok with me. In a world filled with storm, complaint, and temptation, I find supreme solace in those timeless moments that at first glance seem quite ordinary. Could it be that mine is a charmed life? You bet it is. Thank you very much.

Gratitude is the great multiplier. It lifts our energy and steers us away from the darkness of financial worry smack dab into the light of abundance. When we overflow with deep appreciation, we turn a house into a castle, a meal into a grand feast, a job into the source of fulfilling contentment. It's gratitude that holds us together when everything around us is falling apart.

Our soul becomes connected to God through effortless prayers of gratitude that complete the circle of love. When we focus on the many blessings with which we've been bestowed, we do a joyful dance with Spirit as we allow each moment to unfold in its own beauty, in its own perfection.

When you are determined to find blessings everywhere, blessings are just as determined to find you. Every time we acknowledge or appreciate someone and something, we draw more of that to us. Would you really like to know how to transcend and transform your finances? Compliment, honor, acknowledge, slather your love on and extend your deepest and most sincere thanks to every person and every thing whenever possible.

It's easy to be grateful when there's money in the bank and we're flying high in the jet stream of life. When our dreams have been dashed and we've chucked all hope out the door not knowing how the bills are going to get paid, being thankful is the last way we want to be. We're too steeped in the staunching capacity of negative turmoil. These become the defining moments in our lives. Choosing gratitude gifts us with a sublime renewal in our spirit that richly bestows the power to continue upward once again. Gratitude reassures us that there is a landscape larger than the one we can see. The time to begin being grateful is now. Not tomorrow or next week, after the raging storm passes. Right here, right now.

When you permit your mind to dwell on what isn't working in your life, you begin to lose ground. Before I started taking on this work, I didn't like what my life looked like. I didn't even like what I physically looked like. Inadvertently, I had become the author of my own misfortune. The way I dressed, the way I carried myself, and who I was being back then is a stark contrast to who I am now. When I see pictures of my former self from that phase in my life, I barely recognize her.

I was living in a tiny town, population 3,900. I felt like an outsider. Most of the town's residents were born and raised there and left city limits to shop at the mall 20 miles away or attend their kid's sporting events. I had never been lonelier. I had no friends, and I sure did cry a lot. I was sure my divorce was the topic of gossip in various social circles in town. I felt bruised and battered by the tailspin of hopelessness. I wanted to be confident but didn't know how. I had no idea what I wanted to do with my life and felt blazing concern that the divorce would cause our children to suffer; not just emotionally, but financially, as well. I was in the biggest funk of my life, and there was no end in sight.

One hot summer night, I looked up asking for help. Driven witless by sorrow and emotionally drained from the cowering, I hoped someone up there could decode the S.O.S. through my sobs. And out it came. Despite such despair, I siphoned a litany of gratitude for every single thing that I could think of. I imagine that gratitude offered in the depths of hopelessness is the most beloved. Within minutes, I was pacified with an overwhelming sense of peacefulness and contentment. I slept better that night than I had in years.

The next morning I awoke to an earth-shattering "aha" moment, an epiphany that resonated on the deepest level of my core. Gone was the sadness, depression, and hopelessness. The trajectory of my being had been shifted with monumental force. The heavy fog had lifted, and with full mental clarity, I knew well my course of action. I'd read the books-scores of them. I had everything I needed to generate a life of my own deliberate creation. What was missing was a routine. I could hear Heaven applauding me. I felt a band of 10,000 angels pulling me forward. No more stumbling around in the dark living a life by default. My accelerated course work began.

I removed myself from much social interaction of any kind. Since I hadn't felt like I fit in or had any friends to begin with, this wasn't difficult to do. When I wasn't occupied with the care of my kids, I took advantage of my solitude to fully focus on this work. It was only when I intentionally sought out the sacred in the ordinary and said *"thank you"* to it all that I discovered the transformative force of gratitude. In gratitude, I finally learned to love all that I'd been telling myself was not loveable-my body, my nose, my hair, my laugh, and my big beautiful life. I was learning the art of truly loving myself, and the constraints of my self-imposed limitations began to lift.

Possibility oozed from my pores. I made a Vision Board filled with images of what I wanted my life to look like, and I made the decision that I would only buy what I wasn't willing to live without. I weeded everything out of my house that I didn't absolutely love. I imagined myself happy, content, and confident, living the life depicted in the images on my Vision Board. That poster board was now beginning to tell the riveting tale about the extraordinary woman who created it. All I truly ever needed was the profound appreciation of everything I already had.

Louise Hay, my positive thought guru and author of many of the books I devoured during that radical period of my life, convinced me that by affirming, *"I love and approve of myself,"* my world would radically change for the better. Boy, did it ever. That affirmation was everywhere-on my mirrors, in my kitchen, in my car, and in my wallet. *"I love and approve of myself* "became my mantra du jour. The passionate pursuit of my dreams sent my soul soaring. This was my life, my design, and it just kept getting better and better.

You're in the midst of creating a life story with marvelous box-office-hit-movie possibilities. What do you want your life to look like? What do you physically want to look like? Who do you really want to be? You choose it all, and you choose constantly. You're meant to have something better, something richer, something extraordinary. Offer up a high-octane bounty of gratitude often and abundance will erupt on a grand scale. Being intensely grateful is thanking God in advance for that which you are intentionally creating *before* it appears. It is here you'll gain momentum in this work.

Shift your consciousness away from what's wrong with yourself, those around you, and the world, and begin to see what's right, beautiful, and wondrous. You must act as if you are entitled to all the beauty and abundance of the universe, and that it is pouring forth in unlimited measure until it begins to happen. You have substance, grace and style. For you, rapture knows no boundary. Keep gratitude and appreciation strong and constant in your creation of prosperity, and divine forces at work behind the scenes will do the rest. You won't need to struggle or work hard to get it. *It will be drawn to you.* And it may not look like what you expect. No, no, my crumpet. It will be extraordinarily better.

My life is filled with success and prosperity.

Good fortune finds me wherever I am.

Thank you, God.

> "When you are grateful, fear disappears and abundance appears."
> **-Tony Robbins**

> "Gratitude helps you to grow and expand; gratitude brings joy and laughter into your life and into the lives of all those around you."
> **-Eileen Caddy**

> "Gratitude bestows reverence, allowing us to encounter everyday epiphanies, those transcendent moments of awe that change forever how we experience life and the world."
> **-John Milton**

I now easily and effortlessly earn over $_____ each year.

I tap into my creative power daily.

TODAY'S GOALS

You are destined for greatness, so be great today in every area of your life. While you're at it, create order in your world; order lays the groundwork for the beautiful new life you're creating.

_____
_____
_____
_____

THINGS FOR WHICH I'M GRATEFUL

Focus on the abundance you already have in your life and give thanks for it. Be joyful about what you have. Shift your focus away from what's wrong with yourself, others, and the world, and begin to see what's right, wondrous, and beautiful.

_____
_____
_____

AFFIRMATIONS
I am ridiculously happy!

Day 33 - A New View, A New You. Tah-Dah!

"Don't waste your time taking anything personally. Whatever people say about you is just a projection of their image of you. It has nothing to do with you."~Don Miguel Ruiz

We've created our lives to be such a flurry of nerve-racking activity that the world passes us by in a blur. Oh, the rotten angst we feel when the car is acting up...again, and the electric bill is overdue... again. The phone rings and we cringe that it might be more bad news. We look around and all we see is failure. We nurse our grievances like an old war injury. It's over the top. Too much to bear. This has become the dominant groove that we subsist on. Our guts ache from the worry we feel, and we want to run in the other direction and escape into a world where we don't have to be responsible for any of it. We're on a constant lookout for what's wrong, instead of what's right. Our glass is always half-empty. Our lives are so hard and so full of complaint that we can hardly stand ourselves any longer. Cursed? Hold on. Wait a minute. You're simply experiencing the results of your own mental mis-creation, and the main ingredient is your point of view.

I have seen plenty of dark nights and have lived to see another day. It's all an illusion, but we can see it differently, if we choose. Once we shift our view, we shift our experience of it. When all seems lost, an opportunity exists to find hope and the perfect resolution. We make everything so dang significant. We are meaning-making machines. It's what human beings do. We attach meaning to everything. We make absolutely everything mean something.

You want to be in relationship. You go on a date and have a wonderful time. This guy is great, you tell yourself. You're sure he'll call the next day. He's so taken with you that you're sure he won't even wait that long to call. He'll call that night just to be sure you arrived home safely. You grow excited and start imagining what life will be like with this wonderful man. You can see yourself growing old together. Days pass, you don't hear from him, and your hopes are dashed once again. You hate yourself for making such a bad first impression. You spend the next few weeks beating yourself up for not being pretty enough, thin enough, funny enough, whatever enough. Then you turn your hatred on him and think he's such a jerk. You didn't think he was that great anyway. And it's a good thing you found out early on just how much of a jerk he really is. You become irritable with those closest to you and say awful things to them so they can feel as badly as you do. Now you're not sleeping well either. Your mind can't stop perseverating on that first date.

Your brain is sending you data from all the past relationships you've ever been in, and it colors your view of the recent date. The data it sends are the failures, heartaches, and shutdowns you experienced from previous relationships, which make it difficult to be fully present in the experience you're having now. Weeks later, you run into the jerk you had dinner with, and he seems happy to see you. *"What does he want from me?"* you suspiciously ask yourself. He proceeds to say he's sorry he didn't call, but he lost his cell phone somewhere between the restaurant and his house the night of our date and had no idea how to reach you. *"Yeah, right. He's lying,"* you tell yourself. He then says he'd really like to go out again and asks if you'd like to have dinner that night. Boom! You're back on a high again, and on and on it goes. Ugh. The energy wasted beating ourselves up and making him wrong for not following your rules was all in vain. And we wonder why we're not in a relationship.

We do this all the time. Our every experience is subject to our own filters, distortions, and view. The human brain is constantly assessing, assuming, and judging everyone and everything, and it's all memory based. The brain stores the memory of thousands of experience we've had. It pulls the data from a past experience to respond to a similar experience we're currently having. This is how the brain operates, and everyone we encounter has a brain that is doing the very same thing. The emotional teeter-totter we're on distracts us from creating a life we love. We're in our heads far too much, and that's never, ever a good place to be. The brain is always projecting the past into our future. It's what the brain does. Allowing ourselves to be in the here and now, to be fully present, is what redeems us from emotional drainage. When we transmit our energy in so many different directions, we lose our ability to concentrate well. Focusing on prosperity becomes the furthest thing from our mind, so abundance never arrives.

Our view is entirely made up, and so is everyone else's. Nothing anyone says to us causes us to feel badly. We are choosing to feel badly about whatever it is they said. Others are simply operating from their own brain pattern, from their own point of view, just as we are. We attach meaning to whatever it is they said that caused our emotional reaction. Take charge of your emotional reactions and stop taking things so personally. There is no good or bad situation. The situation is simply a situation. It's only when we view a situation as 'bad' that the situation turns out to be bad. Your view of money and finances is the result of what you believe about it. We suffer over the car that won't start or the bloated bill that arrives, but suffering is completely unnecessary. Emotional suffering is a response that is chosen. The purpose of the soul is to express itself while in a human body. If we remembered who we really are and became the demonstration of that on a daily basis, we would end all fear and worry. No situation would be viewed as a problem.

If you want to catapult your finances to the next level, change your view of any situation that causes emotional suffering. Think, speak, feel, and act as the divinity you are within. God exists in all circumstances. See the divine in the car that won't start, and the struggle disappears. When you choose to live from this vantage point, money circumstances- every one of them- become blessings instead.

Our minds can carry so much pollution if we're not watchful. We're creating prosperity, and anything negative hanging out in our space undercuts our cosmic capabilities. We invoke our world through our view of it. Changing our perspective matters. We can see the glass as half full and give thanks and blessings for that half-filled glass. Yes, we want a full glass, and we may be disappointed that it's half empty, but celebrating the half that we do have fuels the energy of creation. It's all energy, and the energy we project is the energy we receive. We become vastly powerful once we become adept at perception management and choose to have a priceless view of reality.

Once we choose to see the unimagined capacities for courage, compassion, and love within ourselves, we are able to recognize it in others. Projecting negativity through our thoughts, emotions, and spoken words is like spreading an infection, only we're the ones who become incapacitated. It's all mismanaged brain patterns. Quiet yourself and go within and then come from within when you're dealing with the outside world. Allow your soul to respond for you.

Stay out of your head. It's dangerous in there. Otherwise, you wind up over-analyzing, over-thinking, over- assuming all over the place. Shift your focus, and you change your world. Feelings of loneliness don't mean you're actually alone. Seek evidence of love and success and it will be drawn to you. Look for the greatness in others, and you find will it. Slather life with your love and admiration. When you enter a room of strangers, see friends instead and friends they will become. The next time you see yourself as guilty, choose to see your innocence. Look only to yourself to be happy, and let everyone else off the hook, for Pete's sake. No one is responsible for your happiness but you. Take stock of every single blessing right in front, back, and beside you. I assure you, there are many.

You're waking up with a whole new view. You're wearing rose-colored glasses, so take a good glance around. You see through new eyes that look for the bright side in every single situation. You're training yourself to shift your focus from not enough to more than enough. Your cup runneth over, and you can change your direction at will. Life is most certainly what you choose it to be. After all, you can do magic.

You are being propelled toward a more noble perfection as surely as the sun pulls a flower towards its light. Your ethereal soul is calling you to a potential not yet realized. You woke up this morning and were graciously given the precious gift of another day. Many others were not. Go now and amaze yourself. It's such a good life!

I feel it. I believe it. I achieve it.

I choose who I am in the world. I am extraordinary.

I automatically focus on the positive.

> "Things do not have meaning.
> We assign meaning to everything."
> **– Tony Robbins**

> "You cannot control what happens to you, but you can control your attitude toward what happens to you, and in that, you will be mastering change rather than allowing it to master you."
> **-Brian Tracey**

I now easily and effortlessly earn over $_____each year.

My soul is pure joy. I allow it to come out and play each day.

TODAY'S GOALS
Practice being happy today. I mean *really* happy.

_____   _____
_____   _____
_____   _____
_____   _____

THINGS FOR WHICH I'M GRATEFUL
As surely as the snow falls and the stars twinkle in the night sky, your dreams are coming to life. You are so loved.

_____   _____
_____   _____
_____   _____

AFFIRMATIONS
Concentrate on prosperity. It never fails. Ever. Now generate some love and joy.
Next, allow all the magic to arise.

_____
_____
_____
_____
_____
_____
_____
_____
_____
_____

Day 34 - The 50-Million-Dollar Race Horse

"The last three or four reps is what makes the muscle grow. This area of pain divides the champion from someone else who is not a champion. That's what most people lack, having the guts to go on and just say they'll go through the pain no matter what happens. " -Arnold Schwarzenegger

Behind every great legend lies a tale of faith, determination, discipline, and pure, unbridled passion. Secretariat was an American Thoroughbred and considered the greatest racehorse of all time. His owner was a housewife named Penny Cheney, a woman who daftly maneuvered the aggressive, male-dominated world of horse racing and risked everything to make her horse a valiant champion. And a true champion he was. Surmounting all disbelief of promise, he grew to be a race horse of the highest achievement. He ran as though he had an appointment with destiny, and he certainly didn't want to leave destiny waiting. He galloped to greatness when he won the Triple Crown in 1973 and crossed the finish line by a record breaking margin-a mind-blowing 31 lengths. His was a story of hope, heart, and courage. Following his death, an autopsy revealed that Secretariat's heart was the largest heart in racing history; nearly three times the size of other race horses. Many made up their minds that the horse was born with an enlarged heart and merely fulfilled on his natural born gift. But those who knew the charismatic Secretariat felt very differently, and believed his strong will and determination to win not only strengthened his heart but enlarged it into the massive high-caliber performing engine it needed to be to fulfill on his promise.

When my friend Jody shared with me a mind strategy called "The 50 Million Dollar Race Horse", my ears perked up. This was a life changer for me. She told me one of her friends had created an inspiring way to bring intentionality to all areas of her life and it goes something like this: if you own a 50-million-dollar racehorse, you take measures to ensure your investment is given exceptional attention so it performs like a champion every time he runs out of the gate. Even the most infinitesimal details of the horse's care are well thought out and planned. It's fed the most nutritional grains; the stall is kept immaculate. He's given the best veterinary care available and gets plenty of sleep and water. He is properly groomed; his hooves well-maintained. The very best trainers are brought in to develop the horse's potential through rigorous and consistent training. Great care is given to expertly shod the horse so it does not become agitated or uncomfortable. The 50-million-dollar racehorse is meticulously groomed for triumph. He is applauded, encouraged, respected, and loved as he is conditioned for peak performance to win the next big race.

Secretariat was an unwanted colt, and his potential wasn't visible to anyone when Cheney won him in a coin toss. But Cheney had a hunch about that horse, and that hunch paid off handsomely.

I have a hunch about you, you know. What would it look like if you trained and developed yourself like a 50-million-dollar race horse? You *are* a 50-million-dollar racehorse. You are that precious. The fulfillment of your promise, the fulfillment of your every dream, it comes from joy, from emotional freedom as a lifting up to the heavens.

Each one of us has an intended purpose. To reach our God-given potential, we must want it badly enough to develop ourselves daily like a prize-winning racehorse, victorious and looking straight ahead to the Winner's Circle. If we quiet our minds, we can hear our whispering instincts, our internal compass. It's never too late to turn around, re-calculate, and pursue what we believe to be our destiny.

We are in the midst of a beautiful journey-to go beyond ourselves, beyond anything we ever thought possible. We have within us the power for becoming what we were intended to be, and we can no longer squash our instinct.

How we use our gifts determines our rise or our fall. Each one of us has the capacity to create anything we want. There is great wisdom and power within us, but if we want life-altering results there's some effort required. All it takes is concentrated intentional effort to manifest all we desire. With the proper intent and motivation, we take responsibility for our ability to create. We create by the nature of our thoughts, emotions, spoken words, and imaginings. Our concentrated thoughts eventually materialize from imagination to reality. The more positively charged our thoughts, words, and imaginings are, the more joyous our lives become and the bigger the manifestations of our exacting design can become. A simple daily regimen of prayer, meditation, and whatever action calls to us is all that is required to create new circumstances. By taking control of our mind and concentrating our thoughts on what we want to occur for us, like abundance, invisible forces rally on our behalf until abundance pours into our lives.

To be a person of the highest effectiveness, we take advantage of all our faculties to achieve substantial results. Frequent periods of deliberate practice of our mind power equals extraordinary results. It's all about how we train, how we practice. Instead of merely slogging through our affirmations or imaginings, we aim to get better at them. We increase our concentration and focus each time, adding more detail and even more positive emotion.

There are hundreds of reasons we tell ourselves we can't do something. We even tell ourselves we are not worthy of love, respect, and abundance. We are not caring for ourselves like a 50-million-dollar racehorse when we listen to the voices in our mind that perpetuate our suffering. The more we love and accept ourselves, the more we experience nirvana. We are capable of absolutely anything we want to be capable of. It is the voices who say otherwise.

If we persist and refuse to give up, we can overcome anything. How we practice is how we perform. It's akin to an athlete in training who not only sees himself winning, but he feels it, too. Our affirmations are vital to our success, but now we need to move beyond the intentional thoughts and connect to our energy as well. The more energy, emotion, passion, and power we can infuse in this work, the more we can begin to create the big shift in prosperity.

The human mind is fertile ground, and we plant seeds in it continually with our thoughts, emotions, and imaginings. We choose to create and, therefore, experience. We train with a purpose. We concentrate on our goals. We don't waste precious energy dwelling on past mistakes, as this only causes us to feel remorse and unhappiness.

How very prudent it is to take charge of how we spend our time and control even our unimportant, small actions. Having a purpose for everything we do and examining each proposed activity to determine if it adds meaning to our life, or if it is just another empty and meaningless activity void of fulfillment are intentional choices. The mind cannot be disorganized one minute and organized the next. If we allow our mind to wander aimlessly while we're are doing the small tasks, it's more difficult to concentrate on the important actions when they come about.

We can wise up and use even the smallest tasks to expand ourselves with the practice of our mind power. When hectic modern living begins to take its toll and things start going haywire, I don't just sit there. I clean. This is reverent time for me, as I gain hours of peace with my rubber gloves on. These are the minutes of my life used to create the next best thing I want in my life, and for me, it's bliss. I channel my creative energy as I vacuum and scrub floors repeating my affirmations. Some of my most brilliant ideas come when I'm bonding with my Hoover vacuum. It is in cleaning and organizing that I plant in my mind that which I want to grow.

Take a backward glance throughout your journey. No longer are you a spectator in life. You're out of the stands and on the court playing full out. You've mapped out your pending adventure by creating daily goals. However, no matter how badly you want to overcome financial hardship, your hopes will be exterminated if you don't devote the time to practice developing your creative powers.

Don't miss the starting gun. There's no time to dally. Ply your manifestation skills. When the head clatter kicks in, don't add to it. Simply ignore the rumble. Allow your thoughts to graze in a lush pasture of positivity. Be a champion. Be yourself. Begin to groom, train and develop yourself like a 50-million-dollar racehorse. An awe-filled grace filled the skies above when you were born. Reaching your divine potential is a no-brainer. You've got this one handled. Giddy up!

I am a 50-million-dollar race horse. I am destined for greatness.

I am the luckiest person I know.

Good fortune finds me wherever I am.

> "Expect your every need to be met. Expect the answer to every problem, expect abundance on every level. "
> **-Eileen Caddy**

I now easily and effortlessly earn over $_____**each year.**

TODAY'S GOALS

Today, take the actions you've been putting off. Do something BIG! This is *so* your week to shine!

_____ _____

_____ _____

_____ _____

_____ _____

THINGS FOR WHICH I'M GRATEFUL

You're always the first to smile. Ever notice how you light up a room when you enter? Well, you do.

_____ _____

_____ _____

_____ _____

AFFIRMATIONS

Drop all the cautious pessimism and thoroughly enjoy the money fantasies of a lifetime today. Dream BIG!

_____

_____

_____

_____

_____

_____

_____

_____

_____

_____

_____

_____

The meaning of life is for you to give it meaning.

Whatever you decide things mean is how you define your reality.

Day 35 - Clap If You Believe!

"I don't believe. I know." -Carl Jung

How to create absolutely anything in life? Act as if it already exists and don't look back. Can we actually trick the mind into believing something is true and have it actually become true? Yes. We do it all the time. You want evidence? We're already living what we believe. Everything we've told ourselves about our financial circumstances has already come true. If you really want to know what you believe about yourself, your income, your reality, just look at your present circumstances.

A self-fulfilling prophecy means that what we believe to be true will become true because we subconsciously and consciously act in ways that cause events to unfold that are in direct alignment with our beliefs. A firmly held belief has the power to affect and even alter everything it touches. As you believe, it is so. The frequency of energy you emit from your beliefs is transmitted through your thoughts, emotions and imaginings. You'd forgotten how powerful you are. Now you remember. *You become what you believe.* What determines your level of abundance is your reverberation to it. Abundance must occur in your mind before it can manifest in your life.

We cannot lie to the mind, but inundating the brain with seeds of new truths by way of our affirmations is how to foster a new belief system. With repeated affirmations, we can condition the mind into believing something is true until it eventually becomes true for us. If we believe we must work hard to succeed, money will only come to us only if we work hard to get it. If a six-figure income is what you desire, but you wake up each day thinking what a miserable failure you are, and it's impossible for you to create that income. You'll never get it. You'll think of all the reasons why life isn't going your way, how broke you are, and how difficult everything is for you, blah, blah, blah. What you're doing is perpetuating and affirming your lack of a decent income by being such a negative Nelson.

But wait. Let's examine the situation from the opposite angle, shall we? If you want your financial situation to transform, you must begin believing it is already occurring. There can be no doubt when manifesting. Doubt is the enemy of manifestation. Manifesting occurs from knowing exactly what you want. Whatever you know or believe is precisely what you'll experience. Continually acknowledging the presence of prosperity, whether it exists yet or not, and acting as if the creation of prosperity has already been realized, is a potent and highly productive skill to ply. You get what you expect.

Our beliefs attract what we want; our beliefs detract, also. What we give thought to, what we believe to be true, *is* true. Our brains cannot distinguish what is really taking place and what is imagined. Whatever it is you believe about money will be *exactly* what you experience. It all begins with thought. Thoughts, if powerful enough, are accepted and believed by our subconscious mind. This is the way the mind works. We first clearly picture what it is we desire and fully concentrate our attention on it. Having an absolute and unmovable faith that our desire will be realized is our ticket to financial freedom. We feel it in our guts. We feel it in our spleens. We are that certain of the outcome.

Under hypnosis, if a weightlifter is told he is as weak as a toddler, and he won't be able to lift a string to the 100-pound mark that he easily bench pressed prior to being hypnotized. He attempts to lift the string, consciously activating all the appropriate muscles. His subconscious believes that he is weak, so his muscles involuntarily act against him; he's unable to complete the simple lift. Still under hypnosis, he is then told he is stronger than he has ever been. The weight lifter is now able to bench press 200 pounds, exceeding his previous capacity for strength, since his mind believes he is capable of doing so. This is the way the mind works; it believes what it is told if enough intentionality is used.

Your current state of financial affairs is the product of an inherited belief system. Success with manifesting prosperity is dependent on your strategy. Your daily prosperity work is the strategy to help you pay attention to your thoughts, conversations, feelings, and what you're imagining so you easily create a new belief system. Pay close attention to what you pay attention to, and you'll create blessings of the most magical variety. The tools work and will always produce a physical outcome in the world. Like working a muscle, the more you practice it, the better it works for you. Consistent effort yields plenty of prosperity.

We direct our energy into the patterns we believe are possible. If we cannot conceive a thing, we cannot create it. My friend Rebecca told me she was feeling stalled with her work on prosperity, and she finally admitted that she couldn't even fathom the possibility that she was capable of generating an income of $100,000 a year. If you knew Rebecca, you would be quite surprised that such a confident, beautiful, and grounded woman could feel inadequate in any area of her life. Sometimes our programming is so ingrained that we completely stop ourselves, even if every other aspect of our personality has it going on.

If you're anything like Rebecca and you're having a difficult time believing a certain income amount is attainable for you, there are actions you can take to help ease you into this. Mirror work is exceptionally powerful. A few times each day, stand in front of a mirror, look into your beautiful eyes and repeat your money affirmations out loud for a few minutes. This may be very difficult at first, since your old programming is contrary to what you're working towards creating now. Continue to push through any discomfort. Another option is to temporarily lower the amount of the income you desire to an amount that seems less threatening to you. With time, you'll be able to adjust this upwards once you begin to see evidence of your earning potential.

Expect to receive whatever it is you desire. Believe that you now have the income you say you do and you begin the creation of it. Prepare for its arrival on every possible level- material, physical, and spiritual. We don't have to know how it will come into being; we simply trust that it will. Our job is to build the foundation, follow any leads that come our way, and prepare for it. If you want a new car, clean out our garage to make space for a new car. Want a new home? Take a tour of a model home to get the feel of it in order to feed your desire to have a new house.

The universe will always bless you in bigger ways when you least expect it, but impatience can be a secret saboteur. We want prosperity, and we want it now, damn it. Not knowing how or when our prosperity will appear can be very disconcerting. We want in on all the juicy details of the how's and the when's of its delivery, but that's not our job. We're impatient to a fault. We keep prosperity at bay the more we perseverate over it. We want to 'do' something to make it happen faster. All there is to 'do' is continue your daily mind training and fully expect your every desire to manifest. It is only when we surrender the delivery details of our dreams that our every desire or wish can be fulfilled. Believe, imagine, and let go.

Act as if you are entitled to all the beauty and the abundance that exists, and see it pouring forth in unlimited measure until it begins to occur. Maintain an unfaltering belief in your success. You are the master of your own good fortune. Believe that nothing can disturb your peace of mind. Picture what is wanted as already yours, and yours it surely will be. See yourself as you would like to be. Act as if your dreams have already come true and filter every thought and emotion through that view. This is the space you want to inherit, so go there.

We've secretly believed all along. Believe you know all there is to know, and you'll know all there is to know. Simply claim your good-whatever it may be. Claim it verbally and speak into existence that which you want to receive. Charge it with positive emotions and go about your business knowing, without a single solitary shadow of a doubtful doubt, that it is now in the making.

Live a life of exceptional expectation. Expect a miracle, and a miracle shall be. Have profound faith that miracles are possible, even when there seems to be no hope at all. Live your truth. Dare to dream, and, most importantly, *believe*. You influence the future by believing it's already true. The birth of hope. The birth of faith. The ante is being raised, so act and have a lot of faith. Clap if you believe!

I think of the things I want, and I see them as already manifested in my life.

I now receive large sums of money just for being me.

Whatever it is I believe about money always comes true for me. I believe I am abundant.

> "Those who don't believe in magic will never find it."
> **-Roald Dahl**

> "When you expect things to happen – strangely enough – they do happen."
> **– J.P. Morgan**

I now easily and effortlessly earn over $_____**each year.**

Yes, I can.

TODAY'S GOALS
There's never been anyone like you. You are enough.

THINGS FOR WHICH I'M GRATEFUL
You lack nothing.

AFFIRMATIONS
Whenever I am feeling good, I know that I am moving toward prosperity.
Whenever I am feeling bad, I know that I am moving away from prosperity.

Every day in every way, I'm getting better and better and better.

Day 36 - The Emancipation of a Life of Struggle

"Things do not change. We change." -Henry David Thoreau

Life lurches by and trumps around, splintering our dreams. Giving up, ignoring the situation, getting depressed, and blaming others are some of the ways we react to a financial crisis. Giving up means we feel hopeless. Ignoring the situation only leads to further financial disaster. Getting depressed and blaming others is futile.

Throughout the lengthy and painful process of my divorce, I felt like giving into my despair and depression many, many times. Some days I struggled to get out of bed. It seemed like Frank and I were on several battlefields at the same time, and not having any money whatsoever sent me into an exhausting tailspin. I found myself feeling helpless and hopeless on a regular basis.

Filled with disappointments and painful memories, I was terrified of the changes that were inevitable. Fear of the lack of financial resources seemed to send each of my days careening out of control. It wasn't until I conceded that my ability to generate abundance comes from within that I really took on this work. I began to redeem my days once I developed a daily routine of intentionally taking possession of my mind and my emotions to direct them to the dream life that had my name on it.

I carefully chose my thoughts and my conversations. I wrote my affirmations morning and night. I wrote them while I waited in the car for the kids to finish with soccer practice. I slowed my breathing to quiet my mind when I felt like I was ready to jump off a cliff. Several times throughout the day I imagined myself happy and brimming with joy. I devoured even more books on positive thought to continue my ascension from negativity. I was visualizing daily, and a new inner reality was being shaped. Soon the shift began. I felt happier and at peace. Though I still had no job, things began to change quickly. A few months later, the judge ordered Frank to temporarily pay the mortgage and the utilities. Though it was temporary, it provided some emotional relief.

I pressed on with my mind work. There was one delay after another with the divorce hearing, and I really didn't care. To me, it meant I had more time to work on attracting prosperity. Without fail, I practiced each day all I'd read about. There were even more delays with the divorce hearing, all of which I attributed to divine intervention; I had no idea what I would do or could do to earn a living. Synchronicities began to occur, and with them came great momentum in a new direction. An acquaintance of mine told me that the schools were in need of substitute teachers; it paid $75 a day. Since I had a Bachelor's degree, I could substitute teach. I had no idea how to teach anything, but I did it.

A friend I hadn't heard from in years who lived in California called me out of the blue and said she knew an editor at the *Chicago Tribune*. "You should call her. You were a great writer in high school," she urged. *In high school?? Who is she kidding? What a joke. That editor will laugh and hang up on you.* The voices came alive. *Hmmm, I did a short stint as a reporter at a TV station after I graduated from college. Perhaps calling that editor isn't so far-fetched an idea.* A voice of which I was firmly in control was now on loudspeaker. I took a deep breath, assumed Grace Kelly's way of being from the movie *Rear Window*, and made the phone call. With little to no job experience as a writer, I landed a freelance writing position for one of the largest daily newspapers in the nation, and it occurred easily and effortlessly.

My income was steadily increasing, and the synchronicities just kept coming. Our day in court finally arrived. I did a lot of praying and so much work on myself during that time that I knew in my heart that whatever the outcome was of that divorce, I'd be divinely cared for no matter what.

The result of many divorces is that women have no choice but to rely heavily on child support as a sole means of survival. Since most women bear the responsibility of being the primary caretaker of the children, there isn't much opportunity to find a job or a career with a high earning potential. I knew we couldn't survive on child support alone, so I had to find another means of financial support. I'd been reprogramming my mind to attract financial abundance for this reason alone.

When our day in court finally arrived, the judge explained that he'd spent quite some time considering our situation, and he announced his decision. He explained that he felt it was appropriate to award me not only child support, but two year's worth of maintenance...and the maintenance would be an amount larger than the child support. I was stunned. Frank was ready to keel over. We hadn't even made such a request. My attorney looked like a deer in headlights and said he'd never known a judge to be so generous in a divorce proceeding. A week later, I sobbed as I wrote Judge Adcock my sincere and heartfelt letter of appreciation, promising him that he would never regret his decision. I kept my word.

I pursued a Master's degree that enabled me to be a full-time high school teacher. All the while, I continued using the mind tools to generate more prosperity. Eighteen months later, I completed grad school. It was December and not a good time to secure a teaching position, which are typically filled in the early summer. But, lo and behold, I was offered a job at a high school in a town just thirty minutes from where we lived. The position had become available midway through the school year when the teacher I was replacing left unexpectedly. Funny how that worked out perfectly for me, I thought.

My oldest son, Blake was in college and Miles was finishing sixth grade when the next big shift arrived. Miles announced at the dinner table one night that it was time for us to move to Grand Rapids, Michigan. I loved Grand Rapids. My sister and my parents had relocated there years before. It had all the cultural elements of a big city, minus the crime, traffic and the high cost of living. I'd had many conversations in the past with my boys about moving there, but my conversations were always met with resistance, so we stayed where we were. The randomness of Miles' pronouncement had me believe there was something waiting for us there. Three months later, we moved to Grand Rapids. A new destination with new dreams was calling, and I could hear it resonating in my soul.

It is not true that we are powerless and at the mercy of a fate of which we have no control. We control it all. All too often we settle into the patterns we have developed because they feel familiar and safe, or because we simply don't know what to do or how to do it. We radically alter our own reality with intentional effort. Sometimes we need to take a leap of faith and trust that our angels hold the safety net. We all have the divine right not only to be happy and full of joy, but to construct dreams of our own design. I am living proof of this.

There are reasons why you should be very optimistic about your future. For too long you've kept your potential incarcerated. Your efforts are making visible the life you long to experience. Press on and continue to take possession of your mind, and direct it toward greatness. You are much closer to your goal than you realize.

I AM LUCKY!

I automatically focus on the positive.

I always expect great things to occur for me and I am never disappointed.

> "Act as if you've already achieved your goal, and it is yours."
> **-Dr. Robert Anthony**

> "Life's like a movie. Write your own ending. Keep believing, keep pretending."
> **– Jim Henson**

> "Happiness cannot be traveled to, owned, earned, worn or consumed. Happiness is the spiritual experience of living every minute with love, grace, and gratitude."
> **-Dennis Waitley**

I now easily and effortlessly earn over $_____ each year.

TODAY'S GOALS
You get a gold star for today. XOXO

THINGS FOR WHICH I'M GRATEFUL
You've come a long way, baby. You are beautiful. You are adored. You are splendid. You matter.

AFFIRMATIONS
I am always divinely guided.

"Human beings, by changing the inner attitudes of their minds, can change the outer aspects of their lives."
-William James

Day 37 - Lions, and Tigers, and Bears...Oh My!

"At the beginning of the journey, we had boundless energy and made quick progress. But, as we move closer to our core, our hidden beliefs that live in the shadows and secretly call the shots become exposed. They try to convince the ego to bring out the heavy artillery and initiate a take-no-prisoners fight to the finish. What recourse do we have during this dark night of the soul? Let the ego fight. And while it's distracted with its business, let's take every opportunity to go within, to go deeper than ever before, until we're in heaven." -Tami Coyne & Karen Weissman

We've checked into financial rehab, and darned if we haven't noticed we're in far better spirits these days. In fact, we feel great. And then it hits. We wake up frazzled and find ourselves feeling poisoned by the bile of disbelief that anything good will ever come our way. With clenched teeth and tight fists, we're once again embedded in a fault line that generates our doubt of ever being financially blessed. No matter how hard we try, we remain stuck in financial havoc. We are weary from the battle. Mum's the word for those of us currently dwelling in the realm of fear and negativity; we have all been tenants there at one time or another. Reader, meet Resistance-the culprit of your financial purgatory. Up to this point, we have been unaware of its existence. It rears its ugly head from time to time in an attempt to keep us prisoner in a life of struggle. But believe me, we can undo even the messiest and tangled demise. We are where we are in our finances right now, and it's absolutely perfect.

We have ultimate creative control of our lives. When we're stuck in our circumstances, we're simply being met with our resistance to a new brain pattern. The more we resist, the worse we feel. Most of us give up and throw in the towel when we're close to having a breakthrough. We just don't know how close we are. Hold on. Help is on the way.

When we know what we *do* want to occur (abundance) but still focus on what we *don't* want to occur (financial struggle), the perpetrator is resistance. We create negative thought opposition when we want something badly, yet we still place our attention on what we fear. What we're doing is misdirecting our energy with our thoughts, words, emotions, or imaginings, and streaming our energy in opposing directions.

We cannot create a new life of prosperity if we continue to focus on, worry about, or fester over our current life of financial struggle. It should be of no surprise that we experience what we don't want when we're unknowingly giving our attention to the very thing we don't want. When the bills are due and there's not enough money to pay them, we throw ourselves completely out of whack by feeling frightened and fearful and thinking dominant thoughts like, *"I want more money,"* or *"I need more money, NOW!!!."* Or we may be thinking, *"I want to have financial security in my life because I don't want to struggle with my finances any longer."* This only creates competing energies of wanting and worrying by thinking about the thing we want to occur, while also thinking about the thing we don't want to occur. We're stuck in a state of opposing forces, so resistance occurs. When we're resisting, we're attracting. We're pulled between our wanting (a constant flow of money) and what we don't want (the absence or lack of money). There is that which you desire, but what's also there is the lack of it. Without even realizing it, we drift away from prosperity.

Gloomy spirits haunt our house; they haunt our mind. We die dead from carrying such heavy emotional baggage. We simply will not allow another minute of the clatter in our head, so we begin the evacuation process of the thoughts responsible for it all. Our emotions serve as a gentle reminder to examine the content of our mind. When we find ourselves feeling a negative emotion, it will melt away when we gently guide our thoughts in the direction of what it is we want to manifest.

When you are met with resistance, you have the power to shift it. Abundance and lack are parallel realities. By deliberately choosing in which inner reality you dwell, you cause the shift in your outer reality to occur. By deliberately placing your thoughts on what you do want to occur, over time, you change your habit of thought.

It's vital that you continue to take the necessary actions needed to alleviate your current financial situation while you're reprogramming your mind to attract prosperity. I worked three jobs at one point so I would create a constant flow of money to pay my bills. Take whatever actions are needed to get a flow of money moving in your direction. This is a mental process, people, so schedule a set amount of time each day to take the necessary actions to address your current financial situation: calling the bill collectors, looking for part-time jobs, selling some of your possessions, etc. This will be the *only* time during the day that you'll think about your current circumstance. The rest of the time is spent looking into the future of good and plenty.

I have been where you are. I was deeply afraid, not knowing how I would pay my bills. Once I learned about the negative power of resistance, I never again placed my energy in the futility of worry. Simply calm down. Don't worry. To remove resistance from your path, you must raise the frequency of the energy you're transmitting. Put on some protest music and salsa, cha-cha, or hip-hop your way to a finer mood.

We moan and regret the pains and losses in our lives, paying little heed to our many blessings. We focus only on the bad patches, completely oblivious to this exquisite journey that is our birthright. The world around us only mirrors our internal dialogue. If you've struggled financially, it's simply been your poverty identity, the negative money conversations you inherited from others that's been running your goodness into the ground. You are a wildly powerful and creative being, and you'll master your powerful thoughts by *becoming* the master of your thoughts.

Finally, the poverty identity-that fierce old biddy-will soon cease to exist once and for all. You're going to soar very soon, grasshopper.

I am always lucky.

> "You have powers you never dreamed of. You can do things you never thought you could do. There are no limitations in what you can do except the limitations of your own mind."
> **-Darwin P. Kingsley**

I now easily and effortlessly earn over $_____ each year.

I am in full control of my thoughts, emotions and imaginings.

TODAY'S GOALS
Plan your time well. Your massive fortune is just around the bend.

_____   _____
_____   _____
_____   _____
_____   _____

THINGS FOR WHICH I'M GRATEFUL
You are magnetic to money. Bravo!!

_____   _____
_____   _____

AFFIRMATIONS
All of my wishes are now coming true. I am wildly blessed beyond measure.

_____
_____
_____
_____
_____
_____
_____
_____

My emotions are my choice. If I do not choose how I feel, the machine will choose it for me. I choose wisely and choose only emotions that create a life I want to live.

Day 38 - Lighten Up a Little, Will You? Geeze.

"Resistance is thought transformed into feeling. Change the thought that creates the resistance, and there is no more resistance." -Woody Hayes

We are being tested by God this morning. Feeling overwhelmed by outside circumstances brought on by a horrific bout of negativity, we're now itching for the big score. We're up to our eyeballs in debt, and those spiteful bill collectors keep calling, reminding us of our shame. That big financial breakthrough can't get here fast enough. Hurry up already! The mind bred in negative emotion gives birth to demons-the voices of failure and low self-esteem. When we wane in darkness and the inner noise begins to overwhelm, it's time to get back in control.

Unfamiliar terrain can be a grave and fearsome landscape. We find great comfort and security in knowing exactly how things will pan out for us. We're a society of instant gratification seekers. However, we will not gain momentum in our financial quest by feeling like we can't get there fast enough. Our sense of urgency creates a yin-yang effect of opposing forces working against each other, putting a halt on the flow of prosperity. Having the assurance of a known outcome to a situation is a primary need to quiet the concerns of the mortal mind, so we make the mistake of taking it upon ourselves to determine what that outcome shall be.

It's the 'not knowing' that makes us jumpy and tests our patience. Our humanness is at the helm of such thoughts. We crave the comfort of knowing. We become attached to the how's and the when's of our outcomes. Wanting them to look a certain way, we wind up suffocated and trapped in expectation. Most of the time, we have no clue how the story will end, yet we behave as if we have supreme knowledge of precisely what the best ending should be. As King- and Queen-Know-It-Alls, we want to be right in our reign with matters of importance. We want to know *how* our prosperity will manifest, *when* it will arrive, and *what* it will look like right nooowwww!!! The wall of resistance can only crumble once we release our attachment to how abundance is 'supposed' to show up.

We also believe we must make prosperity happen quickly by taking lots of action. But this only stalls our efforts. We spend so much time and energy trying to figure things out that little energy remains to create with our internal power. Trust me. It is the essence within that infuses everything in your life with blessings.

I have news for you. A good number of resolutions to matters of concern appear in ways we never expect. If we stay steady on the course of prosperity by being intentional with our personal power, we can expect an outcome far better than the one we ever imagined. The perfection of such an end result often takes our breath away. It's that gorgeous and stunning.

When I was in the process of reinventing myself, I struggled imagining my dream job. I had a few ideas of what I wanted to do for a living, but visualizing the details of any one of them was difficult. Truth be told, I didn't know what I'd be good at. What was important to me was having a flexible work schedule that allowed me the precious time with my kids, who were growing up so fast. I had no idea what type of job would afford me such a luxury, but this was non-negotiable. Health insurance was a big factor, as well. Out of frustration, I finally released my attachment to what I thought my dream job should look like, and instead I focused on the job's accessories. I came up with a new affirmation that reflected this, and I chanted it often. It went something like this: *I now easily and effortlessly earn over $100,000 at a job I love, with a flexible schedule and great insurance benefits.* And off I went, affirming all over the place, allowing providence to play the leading role. I knew in my soul that every request is responded to; everything I needed for my highest good would appear at the perfect time and in the perfect form.

Michigan was where we were being led, so I immediately began my job search. I had the entire summer to find a job, so I patiently scrutinized all jobs postings, paying more attention to the glamorous ones. I now had some valid work experience, so I knew I was a qualified job candidate. May and June passed and so did July. I applied for job after job, but nothing was opening up.

The summer was quickly passing, and fear began its decent. The voices were brutal. Had it not been for my sister, Amy, my guidepost, I would have jumped ship, threw in the towel, and took a long sabbatical from life. Amy was the earthly angel who championed me when the unforgiving voices came within listening distance. We all need protection from the witches. We all need an Amy when the wickedness in our head looms.

My emotions always stabilized following an Amy pep talk, so I kept on truckin' with my long walks, repeating my affirmations and continuing on with my plans for relocation. August arrived quickly, and school in Grand Rapids would soon start for Miles. The voices of worry, concern and doubt were deafening and flooded my head. I began to doubt my decision to move. After all, *"How could I move?"* the voices kept asking. We hadn't yet sold our house in Illinois, and I had no job waiting. *"I'm being irresponsible. I'm going to fail. I can't do this. I always make the worst decisions. Everyone will know I'm a fraud. I'm terrified."* I was a black hole that swallowed light, and I could feel the hairline fracture of stress in my head.

But Miles was excited about the new venture. He was counting on me to create a miracle. Oh, the pressure! So here's what I did: instead of allowing the self-defeatist voices to get the best of me, Miles became my anchor to steady me in my manifestation efforts. I would not disappoint my son. No way, Jose. The divorce had already been a painful jolt to his childhood. I would not allow another interruption to his sublime purity and innocence. I pressed on religiously in pure faith of this powerful work. I invested even more time in my imagination, and I kicked into overdrive with the affirmations. I calmed myself as I sat by the lake, allowing the powers of wonder and love to cloak me until the negativity and resistance melted away. And I called upon every angel within a two million mile radius to come to our aid.

Finally, it hit. I received a phone call in late August from a company that wanted to interview me for a position I didn't even remember applying for. I'd applied for a hundred jobs in Grand Rapids, but this one wasn't ringing a bell. *"How on earth could I not remember applying for the one job that actually expressed some interest in me? What's wrong with me? I'm such an idiot. I finally got an interview and I don't even remember applying for the job."* The voices never take a day off, do they? It didn't matter. I'd practiced rising above them enough that I was getting better at ignoring them.

I was offered the position after the second interview, but there was so much doubt in my head I wasn't certain I should take it. Though I was relieved to finally have a job offer, this one didn't appeal to me whatsoever. It was far off my job radar. In fact, I had absolutely no idea what the position entailed. But I was told during the second interview that the income could be lucrative. In all honesty, I was scared I'd fail, so my father stepped up to the coaching plate, since Amy wasn't available to talk me down from the tree I was swinging from. I accepted the position, trusting that divinity wouldn't let me down.

And guess what, little lads and lassies? The job, of which I was so unsure, provided me with an income that was four times the amount I'd made as a high school English teacher. With it also came the flexible work schedule and the insurance benefits I'd been affirming and visualizing all along. Who knew? (My guardian angels knew, I suspect.)

The voices of doom, doubt, and derision will seduce us into giving up on our dreams. They will always be there trying to force us right out of the game we're playing. They are a product of the human mind. Theirs is a desperate mission to destroy us; else they lose what little control they have over us. You hear them begin their tirade, but you pay no attention to their ranting. Even in the face of no agreement, keep the faith and release your attachment to how abundance will appear for you. Once you make a request for prosperity, the universe begins the creation of it.

I am truly blessed.

I have more than enough money to live the life of my dreams.

> "Begin today. Declare out loud to the universe that you are willing to let go of struggle and eager to learn through joy."
> **-Sarah Ban Breathnach**

> "Why are we masters of our fate, the captains of our souls? Because we have the power to control our thoughts, our attitudes. That is why many people live in the withering negative world. That is why many people live in the Positive Faith world."
> **- Alfred A. Montapert**

I now easily and effortlessly earn over $_____ each year.

Beautiful experiences permeate my life on a daily basis.

TODAY'S GOALS

You are your own brand of chirpy elegance. People are drawn to your stunning personality.

_____   _____
_____   _____
_____   _____
_____   _____

THINGS FOR WHICH I'M GRATEFUL

I always have positive expectations. As a result, everything always unfolds for me perfectly.

_____   _____
_____   _____
_____   _____
_____   _____

AFFIRMATIONS

My life is beautiful. It's stunning, actually. And it just keeps getting bigger and better.

_____
_____
_____
_____
_____
_____
_____
_____
_____

I love and approve of myself. Big time!

Day 39- Becoming a Pollyanna

"If you look for the bad in people you're sure to find it, so look for the good in them instead."- Pollyanna Whittier

Pollyanna is the heartwarming story of a girl with a sunny personality and a sincere, sympathetic soul. Pollyanna had an important message for all of us about the power of positive thinking, the value of trust and the significant cost of failure.

My grandmother was a true blue Pollyanna. She role-modeled love and joy all over the place, oozing kindness straight out of her pores and into the neighborhoods of South Chicago. It's no wonder that she is still one of the people I admire the most. Yet her life hadn't been an easy one. The Great Depression and her husband's drinking both had a hand in the meager state of domestic economies in the Moreland household. But that never put a lid on the sunshine that followed her everywhere she went. Her appreciation of moments that yielded even the smallest of blessings were always in surplus. As a child, staying a week or so at my grandparents' house was as good as peeling a sun burn. Her sense of humor was second to none. To me, she was like another kid, easy breezy to be around and fun to the max. The phone would ring and she'd say, *"I'll answer it. It might be someone wanting to give me a million dollars. Helloooooo!"* This was the woman who invented hugs. She was a full expression of pure unabashed joy, and people were drawn to her, even 'bad' people.

Hispanic gangs, like the EL Rukns and the Latin Kings, were always visible in her neighborhood. They were awfully intimidating to an adult, let alone a child. Billy Boy was my grandmother's German Shepherd, and he was as gentle as a summer breeze. Our evening walks with Billy Boy made us an easy target for all those dangers that hide in the dark. El Rukns and Latin Kings included-but my grandmother never feared them. Why would she? Those gangs treated her like she was the General of the World, the Ambassador of Gang Bangers. She was movie-star delectable in their eyes, and now I know why. She treated them with the love, kindness and reverence that went missing in their own childhoods.

My grandmother was relentless in her pursuit of happiness. Every time she found a penny on the sidewalk during our Billy Boy walks, she'd gleefully hark, *"Find a penny, pick it up, and all day long you'll have good luck."* To this day, whenever I come across a penny on the sidewalk, I think of her as I retrieve my riches. I'm reminded that life is meant to be joyful, that there is divine in the ordinary, and small gifts are everywhere if our eyes are open to seeing them. Those who leave a mark on our soul are those who have dared to step out on the skinny branches to embrace their divinity by shining light where darkness looms. Thank you, Grandma Dorothy.

Life is not meant to be a struggle. Our lives are intended to flow with freedom and ease. Anything contrary to this interferes with who we really are. We've all experienced agonizing growing pains, but growth does not have to be painful. Every bad feeling, crisis, or struggle occurs when we are out of alignment with who we really are. We are an extension of God, who experiences through us, in us, and because of us. Our purpose is to experience joy. We are meant to live an expansive, exciting, and happy existence. We were born to thrive. God designed the human mind to be the corridor through which our creative powers flow. We are all vessels of love and light. The essence of who we are is imprinted within our soul, and the ability to create is in our mind. We have been pretending otherwise, and it's time to reclaim our power.

Within us lie the greatest spiritual truths. We have been unaware of our mystical nature. Now we know, and we can no longer deny the revelations of our spiritual DNA. Once we know this, it is impossible for us to unknow it. We have been afraid to open the door to possibility. Many go their entire lives allowing fear to stop them from turning the door knob. But not us. We've opened the door, and the profundities of the ages have flooded our mind. There's no going back.

It makes no difference how many times you've failed in the past. It means absolutely nothing. Every moment is a new beginning. There is no need to wait until tomorrow to reverse the situation. The power to change any situation is now. Your 'somewhere over the rainbow' is right here, right now. You may struggle and feel imperfect. You may have bad days. But each day is a new day, and your attitude can make an enormous difference in how you respond to any negativity you may be experiencing.

When you decide someone has done something to make you unhappy, all you're doing is giving away your power by using them as an excuse to not feel good. Where we place our focus always determines our response. In life, we're going to have encounters with some very angry and negative people. There's no avoiding it, but how we participate in that interaction is completely up to us. We can choose to make a difference by passing along something good to someone else. Choose to see each person who irritates you through the eyes of Spirit. Knowing that we were all created by God and we come from the same ethereal place, we see what we can do to help, heal or assist them. Above all else, we can extend our love outward to them, blessing them with the magical powers at our command.

You are the conduit for the explosion of life. Love is the greatest expression of the light within pouring through your powerful mind, creating the world in which you live. Leave this world with more light than you came in with, tender heart. Be kind and love those who didn't know any better, but who are better because you were here.

You've been applying a superb evolutionary strategy to recondition your mind to attract prosperity. Your negativity is becoming less and less comfortable for you to bear. Intentionality will get you anywhere you want to go. These days, feelings of love, joy, and wonder have become your fast friends. Your joy happens in the moment. When you place specific intention and the power of your focus on that which you desire, you bring the true resonance of love and joy into play to create your every wish. When you encounter defeat, pain, and suffering choose love rather than self-pity. When you encounter anger, mayhem, and hate, choose love over retaliation. Never sit down and complain of the adversity; think how mighty fine the pleasant stretches were. Look into your future with excitement and eagerness and see the smooth plains that are right in front of you, and do not let a setback stop you! Think of it as a mere incident that must be overcome before you can reach your goal. Focus on the best things about your circumstance as they are right now, and you'll lift yourself immediately.

Remember, your world is exactly what you make of it. Think about where it is you want to be in your life, what you want to have happen, and what you want to have. No matter how monumental the catastrophe or devastation, if you choose the path of love, blessings of the highest measure will always return to you.

You've been given the astonishing gift of one more day. Sigh and sigh often. Not only is it a great stress reliever, but a nice big sigh will powerfully transmit your focused intentions out into the world for manifestation. Go on. Sigh.

What difference will you make in the world today? Dust off your wings and be an open heart allowing love and joy to rule the day. This is where you are meant to be, angel. You're on your own path to put a dent in the world. You're an advanced soul, so cultivate a sense of wonder everywhere you go. Be hungry for an adventure.

What did you say? Your mistakes, flub-ups, and faux pas have you too stunted to be a Pollyanna? Be one anyway, and how adored you will always be.

I AM PROSPERITY.

> "Joy is not in things; it is in us."
> **-Richard Wagner**

> "Everyone has inside of him a piece of good news. The good news is that you don't know how great you can be! How much you can love! How much you can accomplish! And what your potential is!"
> **- Anne Frank**

> "The key is to listen to your heart and let it carry you in the direction of your dreams. I've learned that it's possible to set your sights high and achieve your dreams and do it with integrity, character, and love. And each day that you're moving toward your dreams without compromising who you are, you're winning."
> **– Michael Dell**

I now easily and effortlessly earn over $_____ each year.

TODAY'S GOALS

Seek the wisdom of your soul and allow Divine forces to guide you today. Keep your eyes and ears open. If you feel you should go to a certain place, go. If someone recommends a book to you, read it. Is there a certain movie calling to you? Watch the movie. Be open to it all.

_____   _____
_____   _____
_____   _____
_____   _____

THINGS FOR WHICH I'M GRATEFUL

When doing your prosperity exercises, think F-U-N, will you, please?

_____   _____
_____   _____
_____   _____

AFFIRMATIONS

I create my own reality. I create with my thoughts, spoken words, feelings and imagination.

_____
_____
_____
_____
_____
_____
_____
_____
_____
_____

Day 40 - It's a Wonderful Life

"Every end is new beginning." -Chinese Proverb

We're a secret society of joy seekers, you and I. We know the way to ecstasy as surely as a flower knows in which direction to grow. We share a mystical bond. Created and unconditionally loved by God, we are forever connected. Cosmic soul siblings are we. In quiet stillness, a wondrous power has been gently ebbing and flowing, waiting for its master to take the reins. We realize now the power we're capable of wielding with our magic wands. It comes directly from God.

Love and joy are but sparks of the soul. They provide a telepathic link to who we really are. Once love and joy become your highest priority, you can never go back. The time to remember is now. Always now. How do we keep from forgetting? How do we keep the focus? The answer is simple: seek only joy in life and radiate love from your heart at every turn. These basic truths have taken root within you. Oh, you might forget again. Who you are is so deeply etched on your ethereal memory that all you need to do is allow the great forces of love and joy to cajole your soul into dancing with wild and reckless abandon.

We're at the end of a 40-day voyage. In Biblical numerology, forty is the number connected to periods of waiting, testing, cleansing, purifying, and preparation. Moses took to the mountains for forty days and forty nights, during which he created a two little tablets called the Ten Commandments. After God decided to cleanse the world of evil and start from scratch, Noah and his animal companions (and his family) took to the Arc and escaped the forty days of flood waters. Noah patiently waited another forty days after the flood before he even opened a window in the Ark. David, a small and lowly shepherd boy, defeated the nine-foot-tall mighty Philistine warrior, Goliath, who'd been taunting the Israelites for forty days. After his resurrection, Jesus remained in the world 40 days before his final ascension.

This forty-day cleansing and purification period of the mind has taken you down a very personal and spiritual path to abundance. No longer do you stumble on mis-steps now that you're attuned to Divine guidance. You've peeled away the layers that reveal your long-awaited financial sanity. You know the miracles that are now taking place. You recognize the transformation. You are inexorably changed from the inside out.

You've done well and stayed the course. The adventurer is strong within you. It is the journey that must be savored and fully enjoyed in each moment using all the resources available from within. A sojourner rests well after having known and appreciated the pleasure of a good expedition, always looking ahead to the voyage waiting at the next port.

It hasn't been the cards you've been dealt, but how very well you've played the hand. Just look at you now. You bring forth such an exquisite gift to the world everywhere you go. You've come a long way, baby, from the emotionally out-of-control, worn-out, and worried soul you once were. Who knew it could be so easy to get back on track?

Finally, you have come into your own. Your ship has come in. You have arrived. Forty days ago, you began grooming yourself to better advantage. No longer is life like an open-water swim competition in rough waves. You've accomplished a great deal, you rascal, you. You feel more important to yourself. Ehhhhhhhem. May I be blunt? Well, it's about time! You are no longer blind to your own magnificence, and you're riding the wagon train to riches. Yeeeeee Hawwww!!

Drink in the glorious blessings of your accomplishments. On the plane of manifestation, there is immense value in the efforts you've put forth over these past several weeks. After a bajillion hours of affirmations and self-work, your quest has been fruitful. I am certain of this. You're doing back flips in your head from all the love and joy you're brimming with these days. How immensely powerful you've come to know yourself to be. Are you stoked knowing there's nothing you can't create? Heck, there's nothing you can't do.

In your heart of hearts, you've discovered the pathway to the inexhaustible, invisible well of goodness you've possessed all along. A gathering of unseen forces have all played a part in getting you here. There is so much more available to you than mere mortal eyes can behold. Yours is a life full of promise. What lies ahead is a never-ending fount of ideas and desires you'd like to experience, know, or possess, and the booster rockets you now have on your shoes will take you anywhere you want to go. Allow your heart to lead you and you'll never be lost.

Your determination and commitment are forces to be reckoned with. You are the master of your own destiny, and where you go next is completely up to you. Whatever it is you want to create, you'll do so with lightening speed. There is no limit to the amount of accomplishment, prosperity, and love you'll receive. You now know how your thoughts, intentions, and energy create your reality. You have the technology, so use it.

How courageous you have been. How beautiful you are. There is no one else like you. You are the source of everything. You have the power. Remember always, from the power within all is created.

Filled with such blessing and grace, you dance on starlight-dancing streets. Yours are the tallest and brightest of rainbows imaginable, and a pot of gold will always be waiting for you there.

For far too long, you were conditioned to believe that the external world is more real than the internal world. Thank your lucky stars. They'll be forever guiding you. You were lost. Now the road ahead is clear and life has just begun. Never forget that all you have is all you need. Your emotions serve as your navigation system. Intuition is your compass, and synchronicity is your guiding force. Remember to choose love above anything else. Love is all you need. And joy? Why, joy is your soul's faithful companion. Peace of mind is your most accessible ally, and gratitude will never, ever fail you.

Never be in doubt of where you stand, and where you need to be. Believe. Always believe. Believe in yourself. Believe in the impossibilities no one else dares to seek. All things are possible for the earthly angels who believe. Follow your hunches. Seek God always. You'll find Him in the silence.

You *are* the mystery. Now dreams and destiny await. You have been instilled with such dreams in the first place. You're making plenty of requests of the universe now. It's been waiting to hear them all along. You see, dear angel, you've never been alone. Divine forces have been with you every step of the way. You simply couldn't hear their direction before. Seasoned angels are waiting in the wings, and they are at your beck and call. Rely on them as needed, and they'll lovingly nudge you in the direction you need to go. They'll carry you through the fire every time.

Such wondrous, cosmic forces are wooing and courting you towards something beautiful, amazing, extraordinary, and beautiful from here on out. You feel it deep in your soul. It can be no other way. Your brilliant future is calling. It waits like a lioness in the brush; on her haunches, waiting to take command of the landscape.

It is my greatest hope that you find riches beyond your wildest imaginings, that God's blessings flow to you and yours in even, unbroken streams of abundance, and that you live a life you absolutely adore. May you always find yourself surrounded by laughter, joy, and plenty of good friends, because you deserve nothing less. Yours *is* a wonderful life. I am so very proud of you. Blessings on your good fortune. All of them. Off you go, my dear sweet beloved friend, off you go.

Nothing but love.

I was born to create.

I am a master of prosperity.

> "Your journey has molded you for your greater good, and it was exactly what it needed to be. Don't think that you've lost time. It took each and every situation you have encountered to bring you to the now. And now is right on time. "
> **-Asha Tyson**

> "Mastery of Intention is a deeply personal process that always occurs in the present. No technology, guru or savior, however advanced, can do for us what only a commitment to evolving and operating out of our own divine consciousness and physiology can achieve. The choice is ours in every now whether to give away our power to something or someone outside ourselves, or to summon the courage, integrity and impeccability to return home by walking the challenging but ultimately enlightening Black Road of Spirit."
> **-Sol Luckman**

I now easily and effortlessly earn over $_____**each year.**

TODAY'S GOALS
The sky is perfect. The ocean is perfect. The cosmos is perfect. And *you* are perfect.

THINGS FOR WHICH I'M GRATEFUL
I am the light!

AFFIRMATIONS

> "From the moment I fell down that rabbit hole, I've been told where I must go and who I must be. I've been shrunk, stretched, scratched, and stuffed into a teapot. I've been accused of being Alice and of not being Alice but this is my dream. I'll decide where it goes from here."
> **-Alice Kingsley, Alice in Wonderland**

About the Author:

Julie Dankovich is the President and Executive Director of Plan 36B, and the founder and facilitator of Prosperity Boot Camp, a revolutionary personal development workshop that causes others to be at the source of their own personal success and financial achievement. Dankovich's unique philosophy adopts new thought provoking approaches to success founded in a variety of disciplines that include neuro-science, psychology, spirituality, and quantum mechanics. Julie has a Masters Degree in Education and is a former educator. She was a journalist for The Chicago Tribune from 1996-2002 and V.P. at Fifth Third Processing Solutions/Vantiv from 2003-2014.

Made in the USA
San Bernardino, CA
05 March 2015